TRUTH IN COMBAT AND LIFE

JAMES CRAVENS

CBII KAI SAI LLC

Copyright © 2022 by James Cravens and CBII Kai Sai LLC

All rights reserved.

No part of this book may be reproduced in any form or by any electronic or mechanical means, including information storage and retrieval systems, without written permission from the author, except for the use of brief quotations in a book review.

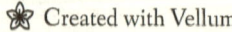 Created with Vellum

PART ONE
BEGINNINGS

CHAPTER 1
INTRODUCTION

AS THE TITLE ASSUMES, this writing is about my journey in martial arts. It is not meant as an autobiography but just touches on the highlights of my martial art journey and the way the path turned and twisted based on my experiences.

This is meant as an easy read and will probably be appreciated by my longtime students and few others. I have certainly not been able to cover everything, but these are the highlights that I recall at this point in time. I hope that for students, they will learn some insights about Chinese Boxing.

At the end of the writing about my journey, I point to how it reinforced my worldview. Through critical thinking and the study of high percentage and probability, the parallel to the metaphysical and spiritual realm was meaningful. The last chapter speaks of this and is, to me, far more important than anything else discussed in the earlier chapters. I welcome feedback.

JAMES CRAVENS

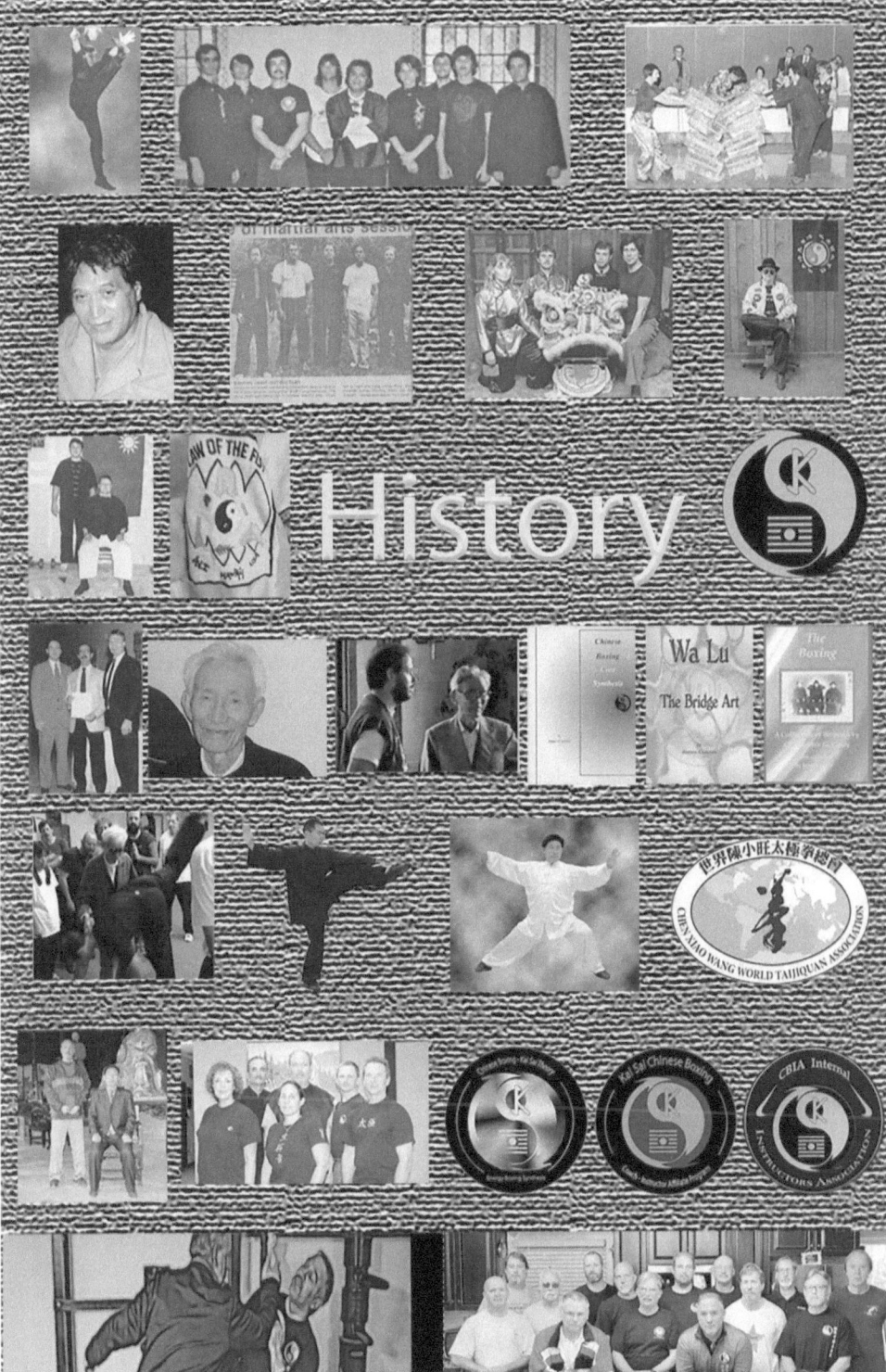

CHAPTER 2
HISTORY

AS OF 2022 my martial art involvement has spanned 59 years. At age 12 I was motivated to start martial arts because of being attacked on the first day that I was coming home from Junior High School. Nothing happened that day, but I asked my Father about self-defense, and he indicated that I should be able to protect myself. I asked him about taking lessons, and he agreed.

My first teacher was some kind of Kung Fu teacher, but my lessons were limited. Later that fall my Dad said there was a Karate Class at the University where he taught. I began going to classes on Saturdays and Mondays. The Karate was a mix of Japanese and Okinawan Karate—a lot of basics and a little bit of Kata or form. The main thing we did was spar; and, after a few months, we began to attend many tournaments.

During the next four years my teachers would change, but I would continue competing in tournaments for the next ten years. Eventually, I became involved with Daniel Pai and the Pailum Association. Pai had an art that he claimed was from his grandfather. I could write volumes about my ten years in this Association. However, I will move on to a teacher named Christopher Casey.

Mr. Casey was one of the more brilliant people I have met in the martial arts world. He was not a gifted athlete, but he had a gifted mind; and what he developed for his martial art was eventually the art I had been looking to learn. It was a realistic study of martial arts. I was used to the tournament fighting, which back then was done with no padding. While there were controls in some of the tournaments as far as contact, most of those we attended were of people trying to knock you out with foot or hand. So the pressure to me was similar to a real fight; but the rules, like in any sport, did not raise the competition to a realistic level.

The problem with realistic fighting is the training. How do you train safely and still be able to understand the violence and effects of real fighting. It takes a lot of effort and creative thinking to address this problem.

Although I studied with Daniel Pai until 1976, I began with Mr. Casey in 1971. Pai encouraged me to go down to Atlanta and learn from Mr. Casey since Pai's way was all about bringing many things into the Pailum study. He used many of his students to do this.

In the beginning, Mr. Casey's biggest contribution to me was learning about chin na and grappling. I was very weak in that area prior to my study with him. After the first few years with Mr. Casey, I began the study of his Chinese Boxing which was a synthesis of Chinese arts, both external and internal. Casey was able to love the styles he studied while objectively developing a fighting art that was efficient and high probability. I had a lot to learn in this new art and was able to study much more with him starting in 1976 when I became his indoor student.

I had to chase him from city to city as he moved around a lot, but he finally settled in Stanford, Connecticut. This is where I had my best training with him. He passed away in 1986. My position as President of the Chinese Boxing Institute International organization that he had started in 1981 continued. He had a board of directors consisting of many of his teachers. After his death, I had to do a lot of thinking to evaluate and make sure I could organize and remember the things that he had taught. So the next four years were critical and important to me as I evaluated and meditated and organized his arts and methods.

I moved to Florida in 1988, a couple of years after Casey's passing. During those years of careful analysis, I began looking for a good internal artist in Chen Style Tai Chi. Mr. Casey had told me to do so, and one just happened to walk in my studio one day. Gaofei Yan gave me a great start to Chen Tai Chi. He was quite knowledgeable and was a good teacher. He introduced me to his teacher, Chen Quanzhong, who stayed with us for about a month during three separate trips to the United States.

After several years, our paths went different directions, and I was able to connect with world famous Chen Xiaowang of Chen Tai Chi. After a time, he made me an indoor student, and I was able to host him in the US around 15 times. He is one of the best at teaching correct internal posture. As one begins to learn the posture and alignment, the next challenge is to move while keeping the same posture. Chen Xiaowang was generous with his time and teaching, and I was able to learn a lot.

As Chen Xiaowang traveled less to the US, I was able to connect with his nephew Chen Bing. Chen Bing was one of the nicest people I have met in the martial arts. I was able to host him for a week in the US maybe a dozen times. He is quite skilled, and one of the best in the Chen Tai Chi Family.

So while this is a very brief overview of my path, I have continued to increase my activity with other seniors my age that teach the internal arts. At the same time, I have maintained enough connections with the younger generation in CBII to keep teaching and coaching the Chinese Boxing method of Mr. Casey. In 2019 I formed an LLC called the Chinese Boxing Instructors Association. The purpose was to encourage growth with the hope that a younger generation could be trained in this unique art. Our goal is to build it up so that here is a strong contingent to carry on our art.

In this brief history, I would be wrong not to give credit to many of my students and colleagues through the years that contributed to helping me get an education with these teachers. I will mention a few, but there are others who might not have stayed with me but also contributed for a time. They are listed below in alphabetical order. Of course, my wife has contributed the most behind the scenes. This year will mark our 50th anniversary. My kids Jason, Carla and Meredith have from time to time contributed to my business as well. They were sometimes unwilling models in my books :)

Alan Baker
Mark Bayne
Greg Beck
Buddy Benford
John Bernazolli
Wallace Berry
Gary Bratt
Allen Brown
Keith Buckhalter
Yamil Cabrera
Anthony Caucci
Pat Crain
Tom Curry
Robin Ellinwood
Nelson Fleming
Lou Gabrielle
Bill Graves
Ray Hager
Jeff Hollar
Melvin Howard
JC Hughes
John Ivey
Brian Kaplan

Bryan Lewis
Sam Locklear
Rick Lupe
Sheridan Lupo
Felice Mandell
Michael McClure
Ken Mills
Harvey Morantz
Earl Morgan
Warren Obenland
Paul Olivas
Michael Parker
Joe Rea Phillips
Frank Pomeranz
Richard Ralston
Rick Schmoyer
John Shea
Ana Shore
Doug Smith
Cameron Tao
Ray Trillet
Johnny Willson
Ken Wingo
John Witherspoon
Mark Yates

The names above either have helped me in a lot of projects through the years or have contributed financially to my journey or have promoted CBII a great deal through their teaching.

A few others that went other directions but contributed significantly to my journey are:

Steve Alsup
Dave and Patti Everett
Gary Huff
Louis Illar

Rick and Gary Laird
Jack Lannom
Karl Milcavage
Dana Miller
Detlef Zimmermann

CHAPTER 3
EARLY TEACHERS

MY EARLY TEACHERS who influenced me from 1965-1968 were Ben Rhodes (Kung Fu), Mike Crane (Different types of Karate and tournament sparring), and Larry Rhinehart (Okinawan Karate). Next, I was influenced for over eight years (1968-1976) by Daniel K. Pai.

Pai was from Hawaii and was an enigma to many people. He was part of US martial art history when there were several what I call "Kings and Kingdoms" in the martial art world. As a 16 year old, I was drawn into this group. Pai was always kind to me personally and never did anything negative to me.

I became dissatisfied with the direction the organization was going and decided to leave in 1976. After going to China with Mr. Pai and the Pailum group, I made my decision to leave. I felt very sad in leaving at the time because I didn't know what my martial art future had in store for me.

Mr. Casey, my new teacher, was brilliant; but at the time, I didn't realize how skillful he was. Studying Kempo from him, I knew that he was rough and that he had a certain amount of skill. When I became his official student, I quickly learned that he was very skillful.

Including the first four years with him in Kempo and Shaolin, I was to have quite a 15-year ride of Martial Art training.

Christopher G. Casey

Mr. Casey was 4th level Black in Kodakan Jujitsu from Henry Okazaki. He was 2nd level in Chinese Hawaiian Kempo and was 4th level Black in Shorinryu Karate. He studied chin na, Wing Chun, Hsing-i and Pakua from a couple of teachers in the states and in Hawaii. Then he made a connection with the Koushu Federation Republic of China and became the liaison officer for the US and later for Europe.

Mr. Casey got into the International Reinsurance business and was able to travel a lot to Asia for his job. These were the years that he began to learn the Chinese Energy Boxing Arts from some well known masters in Taiwan. His central teachers there were Lo Man

Kai (Wing Chun), Tao Ping Siang (Tai Chi and Water boxing), Liao Wu Chang (Monkey Boxing and Fukien White Crane), Shen Mou Hai (Black Shantung Tiger, Lohan, Hsing-i, chin na, Shuai Chaio and other internals) and Wang Shu Shen who taught him Pakua and some Hsing-i. Although he studied other arts with other teachers, the ones mentioned were his central teachers. From Lo Man Kam he received his *Bai Shifu* recognition.

Mr. Casey learned from each person, and his overview of martial arts was forming a cohesive method that he would share over the last years of his young life.

I will not include my later teachers at this point. Next, I will visit a few of the early events in my journey.

CHAPTER 4
TOURNAMENT LIFE

VERY EARLY IN my training (when I was 13) I began to do a lot of sparring. This was while studying with Mike Crane, Larry Rhinehart and Daniel Pai. Sparring was the main thing I focused on in the first ten years.

The kind of sparring was tournament sparring, mostly in tournaments sponsored by the many methods of Karate with a few Korean and kung fu tournaments mixed in. The Korean tournaments were frustrating because of the rules. Some would not call strikes with the hands, and, though some of the kicks would miss by a foot or so, they would call them points, saying it could have hit you if the kicker wanted.

Most of the tournament sparring in which I participated was sponsored by Karate groups. The United States Karate Association was the big deal at that time, and they had a large circuit of tournaments. Though I competed mostly in the southeast, I also traveled to compete in Texas, Oklahoma, Pennsylvania, Connecticut, New York and Mississippi.

Each tournament was unique. Usually, the organizer would call for a Black Belt meeting to discuss the events of the day and explain what the rules would be for sparring. Most would call the rules a light contact competition. This was before the days of safety equipment. Most competitions did not even require a mouth piece. They would say that for the lower belts they could hit lightly to the body but could only come within an inch or so if striking to the head. Brown and Black Belts could hit harder to the body and lightly to the face. Most tournaments used the same rules.

We learned quickly that the rules often didn't mean much. Some judges would call it correctly, but the contact amount would inevitably increase as the tournament progressed. Some judges would call penalties and even give the victim the win if blood were drawn. However, a lot of tournaments just let the intensity of the hits increase and called points with substantial contact. If a strike caused a lot of bleeding, they might warn or disqualify. We were used to all kinds since most directors needed to have all the instructors help judge, and all these judges had their own idea of what the rules should be. It was very difficult to please everyone.

Standing all day to judge caused the guest instructors to get irritated, and many wars of words were fought over these things. The one thing I learned during this time was that if you followed the light contact rules, you would get injured. For example, if you were close or moved in to punch the face, you were supposed to control your punch within an inch or with light contact. The problem was that there were many fighters that when countering would not use control and would hit very hard. We found that unless we hit hard at the face and head when the opponent attacked, we would get hurt and they would not. The referees were often inconsistent, and you had to get 3 out of 5 referees to agree on the same thing.

Tournaments were often blood baths, especially in the higher ranks. After a while, it was what was expected, and we learned to better protect ourselves. In many ways, I liked the heavy contact because you knew what your opponent was going to do, and you could fight accordingly. I felt like the opponent was going to try and knock my head off, so in some ways this was realistic, even more so than what followed with the use of safety equipment and "full contact" in the tournaments. When a bare fist hit a body, it did a lot more than what a glove would do. As long as there were rules and limited techniques allowed, it would always fall short of being realistic; it was a type of game that you would try to get good at in order to win.

Many things done in tournament sparring would get one in trouble in a real fight but would win points in the competition. My nature was to be miserable all day at the tournament while waiting to fight. Then, after about a minute in the ring, my body would release a lot of built-up tension, and I actually enjoyed the fight most of the time.

Ten years of tournaments that covered about a third of the weekends each year constitute a lot of tournaments. When I had my own school, I still was miserable at tournaments until I got to fight; however, I tried to be a good example to the students and act like I was having a lot of fun. Somehow, I knew this didn't make a lot of sense, but there was a belief that the students needed this in order to learn how to fight and to support the tournament circuit.

I will admit that dealing with the nervousness and fighting under pressure and the timing of one's techniques were the good things that are derived from tournament competition. Being hit (assuming you don't get seriously injured) is good because it begins to develop toughness and lets you know you can keep fighting in most circumstances.

As time went on, they began to allow full contact with safety equipment and the rules changed again. During the first few years of the full contact era, the fighters mostly resorted to sloppy boxing. One reason was that when wearing the gloves, punches did not effect the body as much. Eventually, one would hit hard enough to determine a fight, but it really was sloppy. It got better, but no one was satisfied with the results; people wanted to see and do more. So eventually, the Ultimate Fighting Championship (UFC) was developed for cable TV.

The UFC was an eye opener to those who were only stand up fighters. By this time, our group was ingrained in the Chinese Boxing study, so we had to become sensitive to ground technique. While the Gracie family became historically famous for educating many about the grappling skills that could beat the hitting skills, it was still a game with many rules. The rules and environment heavily favored grapplers with the soft surfaces. The rules were to make people safer and prevent barbaric results. Mixed Martial Arts (MMA) almost got nixed at one point when a senator tried to pass legislation to outlaw all MMA events. Many states had already done so, but it didn't happen and the MMA ended up getting popular.

The study of Chinese Boxing was unique. How do we practice with realistic actions when realistic actions cause injury. Mr. Casey was pretty creative, and we have found that we all must be if we are to have effective training of realistic fighting in the study of Chinese Boxing.

The tournament experience also included form competition. Even though my early teachers pushed sparring, I began to get into form competition as well in the middle ranks. It was funny as we did Shaolin Forms and everyone else at the tournament did Karate forms. We thought at the time that we were soft style, but we were primarily hard style. The Chinese forms could look graceful and were generally a lot more entertaining to watch. Often, the people watching the tournament would applaud the performance of these forms much more than the Karate forms. But most of the time, the Karate judges would not give the Chinese Forms a good score. Finally, over time, they awarded a little more credit to those of us doing these forms. Form is a very different pressure than fighting, but it is pressure nonetheless. It teaches one a lot about the mind and the many distractions that can affect performance.

So I had a love/hate relationship with tournaments. I did not like the standing around and waiting or the politics that reigned heavy. At the same time, it did build a camaraderie within the school and could be fun some of the time and could teach lessons in timing and toughness.

Although I don't condemn tournaments, I made the decision

before studying with Casey (around 1976) not to participate and head in the direction of Chinese Boxing study. Such a decision can have an effect on some students. Just like belt ranking, winning a fight or trophy at a tournament can give the impression that one is more than he is as a fighter. If the balance of all these things can be taught and understood, tournaments may work temporarily for some people.

CHAPTER 5
PAILUM

THE PAILUM ORGANIZATION lasted about eight years for me. I was drawn to it because of the charisma and fighting skills of Daniel Pai. He could be a strict task master. He did push me, and I credit him for that.

The theory of Pai's fighting art was similar to the theory of Chinese Kempo. In the years I was with the Pailum group, many instructors came into the system. They brought their background and forms which ended up becoming part of the Pailum Curriculum. I brought several forms into the Pailum curriculum myself—Tiger Crane form, Flowing Motion 1, 2 and 3, Hung Gar's' Taming Tiger and a few others. Mr. Casey had some early connection with the Pailum, not as a member but as an occasional seminar teacher. He brought some of the Okinawa Kempo forms such as Chinese Soft Fist and Cat's play. Many teachers ended up contributing to what was known as the Pailum curriculum at that time.

Casey had an early fascination with Daniel Pai. He was living in the DC area, not far from Richmond, where Pai taught at a school that allowed several teachers to have classes. So they were both teaching at the same place. One thing you can say about Pai is that he is very interesting. Casey decided to take a couple of private lessons from him because he would promise the moon on what he could teach. Casey became skeptical, and for the next few years, he investigated the claims and background of Daniel Pai as time permitted. Casey even tried to help Pai in his early formation of Pailum. But ultimately, in spite of Pai's great talent physically and his powerful charisma, Casey remained a skeptic based on the information from his investigation.

Pai taught a few forms, but they seemed to be on the fly. He could never remember them the same way, so it was up to the students that originally learned them to keep some type of consistency in the form. For example, I taught Lau Gar or Flowing Motion 1, 2 and 3. Flowing Motion 1 was used heavily by Pai for a period of time. He had me teach it to his students. But because Pai really didn't have it in his memory, when I returned to the school and saw it several months later, it looked a little different than what I had taught. Some differences were from Pai's corrections, and some were from the fact that this sort of thing normally happens unless there is a strong effort to teach it accurately. Pai was creative. He taught me a couple of forms (Butterfly and Flamingo) that were really strange. The Flamingo had some parts that looked like dancing footwork with almost nothing being done with the hands. It was very long, and I did not have a lot of interest in keeping it up because Pai could not help me remember what he had taught. The Flamingo had over 300 movements.

When he taught me the Butterfly form, he put something like handcuffs on my wrist and taught the form, keeping movement of the hands limited. It was not real long and was very cool at the time. I did keep it up for a while, but I am sure these particular forms were made up on the fly. If he ever taught someone else in the future, these forms would be drastically different.

Pailum had a lot of problems at the time; and since I lived in Tennessee and was only in Hartford in the summers, I was not exposed to a lot of the issues. Over the years the issues became apparent. This was one of the main things that led me away from the organization. I learned a lot in terms of toughness and pushing myself way beyond what I thought I could do. He also understood great timing, and I did benefit from that. I don't know that he could teach it clearly, but he obviously could perform it. Pai was a tremendous motivational instructor. He could be as loud as a drill sergeant, and his booming voice was a powerful motivator.

On two special occasions, one at Fort Bluff in Tennessee and the other at a Pailum camp in New York, I saw him perform some of what he called his Pailum techniques from his grandfather. He had someone punch at him in both situations, and he blocked or evaded before starting a series of combinations. I studied Kempo a long time and enjoyed it, but I have never seen anyone do combinations with the speed, circularity and skill of Mr. Pai. I thought it was unbelievable, and I think that witnessing his skill is what kept me so long in the Pailum. I probably should have left the organization sooner.

I remember that when I went to Casey, he asked me why I studied with Pai. I showed him a film I had at the time that showed Pai doing some of the techniques that I had seen him do at Fort Bluff Camp when he performed with awesome speed and power. I thought Mr. Casey would be very impressed, but he wasn't. I felt he had to be jealous or something. I asked him why he wasn't impressed with what I showed him. He said he did admire the physical skills that Pai had. He then asked me if I had seen any technique in the demo that was unique or something I had never seen. If I broke it down, there wasn't. It was the speed and grace he had shown. But Pai's theory was just like Kempo. Kempo does some kind of defense and then goes in for a rapid fire of combinations. While the combinations are useful in some ways, no one is going to punch and stop so that you can have your opportunity to do these combinations. Fighting is far from that, so over time I realized the truth of what Mr. Casey was teaching. The Kempo also stops the energy from applying the forward pressure and the capture energy taught in Chinese Boxing.

I acknowledge the fact that the time with Pailum was useful for several reasons in forming me as a martial artist. Those that may read this that are in the Pailum will probably be upset with some of the things I have said; however, I have been quite tempered in my comments. I've heard many stories from so many people that had contact with Pai, and many had different experiences with him. After his death, there were three or four people that claimed to be the inherited master of Pailum and claimed that Pai had told them these things. No one can deny what someone said he told them. Every person's experience may have been unique when it comes to this unusual person.

CHAPTER 6
KOUSHU FEDERATION REPUBLIC OF CHINA

THE KOUSHU FEDERATION Republic of China (KFROC) was a branch of the Ministry of Education in Taiwan. In reality, it had no funds to accomplish the purpose of spreading the Chinese Martial Arts around the world.

Casey made contact with the Chief Liaison Officer of the Republic of China in Atlanta, Georgia, in the early 70's. This contact was very important for Mr Casey in setting up the US office for the KFROC in the 70's. This contact provided the connection for him to meet and study with the famous masters I mentioned in a previous chapter. Mr. Casey had money, so he began to give generous donations to the KFROC, and in return they introduced him to famous teachers. For years, Casey promoted the organization in the US by selling memberships and 8 mm films that showed some of the masters in Taiwan. All proceeds went back to the KFROC in Taiwan. This continued until Mr. Casey took a job in Germany in 1980-81. The KFROC had a new leader who was a former General in Taiwan's military. He wanted to set new ground rules and to charge a much higher price for membership, and Mr. Casey was not interested. So Mr. Casey resigned and started the Chinese Boxing Institute International with a well known board of his teachers.

Some of his teachers didn't want him to leave the KFROC; but when they saw he was resolved, they agreed to help him by forming the board of CBII.

Later in the 70's, Mr. Pai had also connected with the Taiwan General Liaison in Atlanta, GA. He was able to get some help from him in organizing the trip to Taiwan in 1976 that was my last experience with the Pailum group. I will talk about that trip in the next chapter.

Pai continued this relationship through the 70's but was unable to get Casey's position. He was able, however, to become an important connection for the Koushu Federation, which had a tournament every two years. They would have one in Taiwan, and the next one would be in another country. So Daniel Pai was able to sponsor a tournament in Hawaii in the late 70's. I was not with the Pailum then and was acting as an assistant to Casey with the US Koushu. I thought Pai was past his bounds, but Casey checked and said that he was authorized to sponsor the tournament in Hawaii.

I cannot tell the story of this tournament here, but I know that a couple of Pai's top people decided to leave the organization at that point. I don't think Pai was able to do much more with the KFROC after that. Casey left the Koushu Federation in 1981. For those who have noticed a Koushu Group up north, this is a different group that began after all of the history I have mentioned. I believe they are a Chinese based Group. I did see one of their tournaments in Baltimore several years ago when visiting Mark Bayne.

Casey told me that the Koushu Federation could not pay their officers, but most of them held other positions in the government and were forced to fill the position on Koushu. Basically all they did was sponsor a tournament every two years and let Casey do the promotion that he did in the US and in Europe for a little while. I received a couple of documents from the KFROC during this time. One was for being the Assistant Koushu Federation Liaison Officer in the USA.

Front Cover of Koushu Book

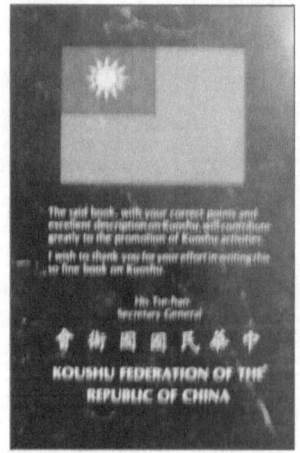

Back of Koushu Book

FOREWORD

I have read your book, Kousho--Chinese Ultimate Mind and Body Discipline. I found from this book one can not only learn the skill of Kousho, but also be aware that the far-reaching philosophy is associated with Kousho. This is one of the best books on Kousho I have ever read. I would like to recommend it to every person who loves Kousho. Enclosed herewith is a separate letter written in Chinese in recognition of your effort exerted in writing this book and great contribution it will give to promotion of Kousho.

HO TSE-HAO
SECRETARY GENERAL
KOUSHU FEDERATION OF
THE REPUBLIC OF CHINA
TAIWAN
AUGUST 23, 1977

Note from Secretary General of Kousho Federation to Casey

T - Author with Chinese Boxing Association, Taiwan: (L to R) Chiao, C.H>, Lo Man Kam, Student, Ho Tse Hao, Author, Wang Shu-chin

Mr. Casey greeted by the KFROC in Taiwan with Wang Shu Shen

CHAPTER 7
1976 TRIP TO TAIWAN & KOUSHU FEDERATION

THE TAIWAN TRIP was a turning point in my martial art career. It is the time I decided to leave Pailum and ask Casey to teach me. I do not regret the trip, but it was a wild ride. It was the year of the 1976 Olympics. We were there in the months of July/August, and it was very hot.

I brought four of my students with me to China. We had no idea what to expect. We had all sent a certain amount of money in advance to Pai. He had worked with the University of Connecticut to do this trip and was able to get the government KFROC of Taiwan to be our host while we were there. We were actually just in Taiwan for two weeks and were to be in Japan for another three weeks. That was sort of strange, but these things were never questioned.

We arrived at Kennedy airport to meet those that were going. There are some negative things about this trip, but I will not tell that story at this time. I will mention one thing that was pretty strange. There were several of Pai's students going on the trip, but there were another six people that were there just to see us off from the airport. Then Pai did a most unusual thing. He told the six students that they were going to come along. They had no luggage, no money and no ticket. Pai took care of that, and we were off.

The two weeks in Taiwan were just great. The host (KFROC) were great and treated us to a great time. We must have had a half dozen huge wonderful meals put on by the host. It was a wonderful introduction into the varied Chinese cuisine.

They also treated us to four martial art demonstrations. In some of them, we performed a little show as well. I had no idea that on this trip I would be meeting some of Casey's famous teachers. I did not even know they were famous when I met them, but it shows that they were closely connected with the KFROC and the events they sponsored. One day while visiting Taiwan's Congressional Hall and Auditorium, I was actually called upon to demonstrate a form. They asked Pai to do something but he would not. Hanging out with Pai always brought surreal experiences.

So I met Liao Wu Chang, who is referred to as the monkey king. He was in his early 80's at the time. He was still around in his 100's when one of my students went to visit some years ago. Liao Wu Chang was from the mainland and had been in the army in his young years. He was something of a hero but had to flee to Taiwan against the incoming government in 1948. When I met him, all the people obviously knew him and gave him great respect.

When Liao demonstrated in one of our exhibitions, he did two amazing things. First he had a bamboo shield and a machete. He did a form. He was very low to the ground and put this shield on top of him as he was very short and flexible. He traveled across the floor in some way, and all you could see was the shield moving. It almost looked like a fast turtle moving across the floor. Once in a while, he would pop up and use the machete for a few cuts and then go back under the shield. He was evidently known for this on the front lines in China—at least that is the legend. He would sneak up and pop up and cut the legs off the horses, knocking the rider to the ground and attacking him.

Either way, he could move in amazing ways in his early 80's. Casey said he had the fastest hands he had ever seen. The other thing he did was a form that looks like Fukien White Crane (Bai Ho

Chuan). Before he did the form, he put a two-inch ball bearing in his mouth and began to push it back and down his throat. He continued to push it down his throat, and it stuck out obviously. Don't know how he did this, but he did the whole form with the huge ball bearing in his throat, taking it out at the end. The full stadium of spectators began to clap and make noise loudly in appreciation.

Liao was such an amazing figure. His teeth were black, but not because they were rotten. He was a traditional doctor that made liniments or jows. He had a black jow that he was famous for and was a big part of his family income. He claimed the jow kept him healthy and caused him to grow very old and stay in good shape. Anyway, there are many stories I could tell, but he is one of Casey's teachers that I met.

I also met Shen Mou Hai, another one of Casey's main teachers. He could do a lot of arts, but Casey wanted to learn the Hsing-i from him. He also learned a lot of chin na and shuai chaio from him.

Shen's demonstration of intensity in chin na reminds me the closest of Casey's chin na intensity more than any of his other teachers.

I also saw Shen do his family art of Black Shantung Tiger when I was there. The style is known for the bobbing head which relates a little to the western boxers bob and weave.

I was in the same room as Lo Man Kam but did not actually meet him. It was later when I viewed my films from the trip, that I noticed Casey's teachers in them.

We left Taiwan in good spirits and went to Japan. It was a long time to be there with no plan, but we did some things of interest. Some of our group went to Mas Oyama's school. All of us went to the Kodakan, the home of Judo in Tokyo. The Judo team was in North America at the Olympics at the time. It was very educational to watch about 30 people training on the mat. Mount Fuji was a highlight for several of my students. We also saw a full two-week season of

Sumo Wrestling. They have about four two-week tournaments a year. There was a giant of a guy from Hawaii named Jesse who had been the first American to win a Sumo tournament. Unfortunately, he lost in a very quick match, his first match in the tournament. We also saw some brutal kick boxing. It was Japanese but was similar to Thai Kick Boxing.

    So the trip came to an end. A lot was going on that I can't discuss, but I did meet with Mr. Pai to tell him I was leaving. On the trip he had actually given some of his main students different positions in the Pailum organization. He was trying to organize things for his return to the states. It was shortly after his return that he moved to Orlando. He put me in charge of Form. He put Clarence in charge of sparring. He put Tiger in charge of the Women's group, and Dave Everett was his right hand man. He even gave my student Tom Curry the title of Comptroller. When I had my talk with Mr. Pai, he was kind; that is the last I saw of him. I had written to Casey from Japan to request that I become his student. When I got back home, I had a cassette tape waiting for me in the mail. It was my "first lesson from Casey."

PART TWO
THE CASEY YEARS

CHAPTER 8
CHRISTOPHER G. CASEY

I MET Mr. Casey in an unusual way. He was researching Daniel Pai at the time. Mr. Casey was born in Atlanta. His mother was a teacher in the school system there and was in charge of special education kids that were gifted. She had two kids that fell into that category, Chris and his sister.

Chris started taking jujitsu when he was about 8 years old. It was his dream as a kid to study martial arts. That study never stopped until his death. He ended up going to college at George Mason University in Washington DC. He wanted to get a masters in Philosophy but could not find a school which would guarantee that he could do his thesis about a balanced philosophy between East and West. Western universities looked down on Eastern Philosophy as a rule at that time, so the Professors to whom he applied to be his sponsors and guides would not agree to his request.

Consequently, he went into the insurance field and worked his way up through various companies and bosses. His desire was to work in a middle management insurance job and spend all his free time studying the martial arts. He said that would have worked, but most of his bosses were stupid; so he just kept going up the ladder, working his way out of middle management. He reached a dead end at the Vice President level, and the work was not interesting to him. He moved to different cities when he took new jobs, so I had to chase him all over the country during the early years. He was in Richmond, Virginia; Atlanta, Georgia; New Orleans, Louisiana; Miami, Florida; and Seattle, Washington. He had made it to the VP level of a couple of companies, but did not particularly enjoy the work. So he went to a company in Seattle, Washington, to study *International Reinsurance*. This was at least a bit more interesting to him, but to him a job was a job. He loved the martial arts and philosophy. He was quite esoteric in his teaching. In the early years, he could be very condescending in communicating with me since I could not always rise to his intellectual level.

Learning international reinsurance got him a great job in Hannover, Germany, where he started a reinsurance division for a large company called Hannover Rhea. He was in Germany a little over a year before heading back to the states to start a subsidiary of the German company in Stanford, Connecticut. He had to be close to New York, the world financial capitol. He stayed in Stanford for many years, and that is where I had my best training with him.

All this time, he was studying martial arts and practicing. He was not physically talented and had only average potential. He pushed himself to get very good physically due to his strong mind. His mind was light years ahead of most of us, and he learned quickly. Then, after studying a variety of arts, he began to put together the ultimate art that would address the questions and problems in realistic fighting. This was his interest.

In philosophy he sought for ultimate truth on the meaning of life, and in martial art he sought for ultimate truth in realistic fighting.

Chris developed what he referred to as energy boxing. In fact, there were many names for his art: Chinese Boxing, energy boxing, Synthetic Apriori Fist (Can you tell he liked philosophy?), Gong Ka (which means "real boxing"), unitary boxing, 6/9 Boxing (changeable), "the boxing," shadow boxing and finally his own name for the complete synthesis—Kai Sai Kung Fu. Kai Sai was a name given to him by a couple of his Chinese teachers. The name Kai Sai meant victorious in all endeavors.

Mr. Casey got a break while living in Atlanta. He met George Hsieh, the liaison officer for the Koushu Federation Republic of China (Taiwan). He taught his son David Hsieh who attended Mr. Casey's martial art club at Georgia Tech University. This is the club where I first studied with Mr. Casey. My teacher, Daniel Pai, referred me to him after I told him I had met Mr. Casey. I didn't know it at the time, but Mr. Casey had run into Daniel Pai in Richmond, Virginia, back when Casey was going to university in DC. They both taught their own classes at a martial art school that housed several teachers. Pai was such an unusual figure that Casey was curious about him. He could see the talent, so when he asked Pai if he knew certain Okinawan systems and forms, Pai would always say he knew everything.

Back to the story of how I met him. I was studying with a teacher in Chattanooga for a couple of years until he moved on from the university. Other teachers came after him, but he continued to call me and make contact from time to time. One day when he was on campus, he ran into a gentleman who was studying and researching the history of Daniel Pai; it was Christopher Casey. Casey was still curious about Pai's background because he made enormous claims about who he was and what he had done. Casey had chased down many of those claims; and since my former teacher had a brief relationship with Mr. Pai, Mr. Casey was there to question him. My former teacher talked with him, but he did not know much of the Pailum curriculum. He called me and said he had someone at the gym who was wanting to view forms and techniques from the Pailum Kung Fu system. I told him I would come to meet him.

I was wide open at the time, willing to talk martial arts with anyone. My former teacher didn't want to show anything, so I started showing Mr. Casey everything. He was very nice, and afterward we went to talk. From that day on, Mr. Casey took an interest in me. He had such gratitude that he invited me to his Georgia Tech club, and I began to travel to Atlanta to study after Mr. Pai gave me the go ahead. Mr. Casey was teaching Chinese Hawaiian Kempo at the time, along with chin na and other things mixed in. He always showed the techniques very powerfully and seemed to want to make sure you believed what he was teaching.

He always asked me why I was studying with Pai. The conversation would sometimes become uncomfortable, but many conversations were uncomfortable with Mr. Casey. He continued to call me even when he moved out of Atlanta until I took the China trip, which was the culmination of my Pailum history. I didn't fully want to leave at the time, but felt I had to. On the question of where I would study next, I thought about Mr. Casey; but I didn't know if he would take on a student. As I mentioned earlier, I wrote him from China and asked to be his student. My interest was because I was always impressed with his jujitsu, chin na and grappling knowledge. I was very weak at the time in that area. So Mr. Casey accepted the request, and I began studying for real. I mentioned earlier that he sent me a cassette tape for my first lesson, and it was very philosophical in nature. It was intriguing to me, but I came to realize that *thinking* was going to be a big part of studying with him. He didn't have a lot of respect for most martial artists, not because he didn't respect their method or skill, but he didn't respect their thinking. It is obvious today that critical thinking has declined considerably in our educational systems. This was one of his strengths and was one of the most important things I learned from him.

Early on, Casey began to teach me some Wing Chun and would occasionally refer to a style called Walu in some of our discussions. I had never heard of Walu and couldn't find any information on it. I tried through several avenues. He had teased me that if I could find anyone to show me a Walu technique, he would teach this art to me. He described it as advanced Kempo at the time. I found a couple of things that I guessed would be like Walu, but it was never accepted. Walu was a family art that was coming from a man he called Pa Ka. He finally decided to teach it to me, but it was something of a process. First, he sent me a film of him doing the curriculum of Walu when he moved to Germany. He demonstrated the applications on Manfred Steiner while Wally Jay looked on. Walu had a lot of curriculum, but the heart of it was the 44 exercises which were purposed to help one learn to move his body in a unitary way. Walu provided more projection and more efficient power. Many of my students were thrilled with this art and still are to this day. It was not a complete art in that it did not have a dueling or a good presentation of needed basics. There were just 44 short exercises, two forms and about 100 techniques to study. At least half of the exercises would probably benefit practitioners regardless of their art.

During the early years I was learning from him, Mr. Casey was beginning to build a relationship with the Koushu Federation in Taiwan due to his meeting George Hsieh. Through this relationship, he was able to do a lot of traveling to Asia, which provided him the martial art studies he wanted. The connection to the Koushu Federation became very beneficial. As I was learning the Kempo, Walu and Wing Chun, Casey was learning many of the other arts he would teach me later, including his "Synthesis Art."

Mr. Casey developed a close relationship with Lo Man Kam and Master Tao Ping Siang. His connections with Shen Mou Hai, Wang Shu Shen, the Fukien Crane teachers and many others were done through a translator since they did not speak any English. He told me at one time that he had built trust with each teacher. In the cases of Lo's Wing Chun, Tao's Tai Chi, Shen's Hsing'i and grappling, and Wang Shu Shen's Pakua, he felt the teachers taught him every thing he had hoped.

In about 1981, Mr. Casey put together the Kai Sai Kung Fu Synthesis. He said that this was not a curriculum that he organized for someone else to teach beginners, etc.; it was a list of his favorite techniques in each category. The categories were supposed to allow one to have a comprehensive study of realistic martial arts.

Casey's other two loves other than martial art were his wife Vickie and philosophy.

He took a sabbatical leave after resigning from Hannover Rhea. He was going to take a year and find a job to his liking. He came back home to Atlanta, and he and his wife bought a nice home just south of Atlanta.

Casey became ill around August of 1986 and passed away in December. He was only 39, and it was a tragedy on several levels. While it was a loss for me, my worldview kept me on an even keel as far as the big picture of life. Many things in life are a mystery. It doesn't mean it is easy, but my faith helped me a lot. At one time, Casey commended me for my faith, saying that it could help me in realistic combat. For those, he said, that believe they are headed for a better place should be able to face a life and death experience with more relaxation and less fear. I think that one can be very scared in a situation without having it related to the fear of dying. Some of my students did not do as well at dealing with Casey's death.,. A couple of students quit practicing the arts. It was and has been very hard on Mr. Casey's family members.

Before covering the time after this loss, I am going to back up a little bit and discuss the arts to which Mr. Casey introduced me.

CHAPTER 9
CHINESE HAWAIIAN KEMPO

DURING THE TIME I studied with Mr. Casey in Atlanta, I invested a lot in the style of Chinese Hawaiian Kempo.

Kempo is a Japanese word that translates "Law of the Fist." The Chinese equivalent is the word Chuan Fa. Our style of Kempo owes its existence to Dr. James Mitose, a noted Japanese minister and Kempo martial artist. Mr. Mitose taught at the old Kapahulu Japanese school in Hawaii. Because of the Chinese influence, we use the name "Chinese." Because of Mr. Mitose, we use the Japanese term "Kempo." And because of where the art was taught, we use the name "Hawaiian"—hence, "Chinese Hawaiian Kempo."

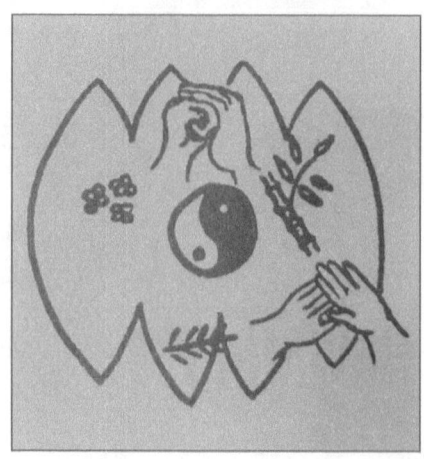

The main Kempo Symbol used by Casey

Some say that the origin of Kempo is from India and was adopted by China, Japan, and Okinawa, where adjustments were made. Others say that Kempo is basically the Shaolin style from China that was reworked some by the Japanese. Dr. Mitose's style is a remote ancestor of Shaolin Chuan Fa. Some say the style was brought from China shortly before 1600. The clan "tong" style of Mitose was known as Kosho-ryu or "Old Pine Tree Style." As taught by Casey, the style included only one form that is known as Monkey Boxing and is quite different from the self-defense techniques. The techniques of the style are precise, quick, and brutal, while the form in comparison is vague, loose, subtle, and flowing in nature. The balance is said to be important in giving one overall fighting skill.

The self-defense techniques teach a combination of throws, locks, breaks, holds, chops, and kicks. The techniques are arranged in eight levels through Black Level, totaling 286 techniques. Casey referred to Walu as Advanced Kempo. I never saw any connection but interpret Casey's statement that Kempo would teach one many combined techniques. The energy taught in Walu based on relaxed unitary power was necessary to take Kempo to a higher level martial art.

Dr. Mitose introduced the *art* to Hawaii in 1929. The school dates back to the 1940s and was called the Official Self-Defense

Club. In the later 1940s, the school became famous as a team toured the Hawaiian islands demonstrating the art of Kempo. Because Mitose felt that the majority of students misrepresented the art, Dr. Mitose quit his involvement in the art and rededicated himself to his religious life. The school was turned over to Thomas S. Young. Young, Mitose's first student, selected Simeon Eli to help in the teaching. Both of them taught classes at the Central Y.M.C.A in Ala Moana. In 1951, the school was turned over to Simeon Eli and moved to his home. The art enjoyed much popularity under Eli.

In 1953, Mr. Eli joined the American Jujitsu Institute (AJI) of Hawaii, the oldest martial arts organization in the United States. Eli was placed in charge of spreading Kempo through the AJI's international organization. Today, the American Jujitsu Institute remains one of the few organizations promoting Kempo and has an unbroken chain of teachers dating back to Mitose.

One day, when I was learning the Kempo from Daniel Pai, I received in the mail a COD box with manuals which had the notes of the first 76 techniques of Casey's Kempo teaching. I was a little shocked. We were told that this was the new Pailum manual for the school curricula. Turned out that many of the Pailum Instructors who lived outside Hartford also received 20 manuals or so. There's a lot more to this story, and I probably should tell it in person rather than in this writing. But I will say that Mr Casey received a copy as well, and he was even more shocked. These were his notes. They were also coded so that it was impossible to know what the technique was by reading the notes unless you had the key words. So Pai had gotten a copy of Casey's notes and was using them to teach techniques. Pai was so creative that he was making up some version of the technique to make a separate curriculum.

So for a while, Casey made a pretty big contribution to the Pailum organization in at least name if not content.

At the time I learned Kempo, it brought me into a closer distance combat mode than I had been studying in Northern and some Southern Shaolin, which is a longer range style that focuses on movement that is large with greater distances in fighting. It also brought some common sense things to self-defense and rapid fire combination techniques. Like many arts, Kempo was not realistic as it was practiced with a person kicking or punching or grabbing before responding and going into pre-arranged combinations. The partner was not to do anything outside throwing the punch/kick or grab. Yet they would think you could get these so fast that it would be a blitz that would be trouble to defend. Of course, there was no sparring using these techniques.

Sparring in the early tournaments was the great equalizer. The rules made it so that when you saw someone spar, it was very difficult to know what style they were. Someone would say they were kung fu or hung gar, but the tournaments quickly synthesized into the techniques that judges would be most likely to call points. It was usually backfist and reverse punches and a few kicks that could hit their target that got calls for points. Then the participants in the tournament would go over to a different area of the tournament and do form competition. It looked totally different from their sparring.

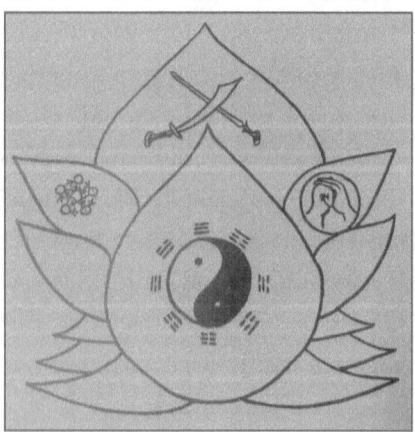

This Symbol combines what I was doing with Pai (the white lotus) and a couple of the Kempo Symbols

Saying all that, Kempo did teach me a lot of movement and was quite interesting. Before I knew better, I started trying to analyze the

Kempo. I thought to myself that it had so many techniques and blocks and strikes, and I was going to separate all these things. I made a list of numerous blocks and then begin to think: *What kind of blocking will I use in real life?* There was no answer in the curriculum; it only offered countless methods with no particular rationale. So when I was shown Wing Chun's simplicity, I began to think of Kempo as being a very unorganized set of martial knowledge. The unorganized part was that it left out a lot of the basics of martial arts to me. It does represent a type of movement, and learning the flowing combinations is valuable.

What Kempo lacks from the Chinese Boxing perspective is the *forward pressure to a finish* idea.

Many people feel that forward pressure means just putting a pressure forward as you deliver your arsenal of technique. This is not the Chinese Boxing forward pressure. Dueling and touch development can be the first place to start applying the forward pressure after learning the basics. Many of the arts that have duels practice them without applying forward pressure. Some do, but we have added a lot of drills for Chinese Boxing in our study of Push Hands, Chi Sao and Joint Hands in order to incorporate the forward pressure into our study. Kempo was a valuable tool along the path, but more integration was needed to be a realistic study.

When Casey referred to Comprehensive Realistic Martial Art, he meant that the art answers all the major questions in combat.

Despite the benefits of Kempo, there are many gaps in the curriculum.

CHAPTER 10
LINK TO WALU

WALU WAS CALLED THE "BRIDGE ART." It focused on 44 exercises that were practiced for five minutes to feel the combination. Several could be cycled smoothly left and right with the end purpose to make one more unitary in their movement. In general, unitary movement makes it possible to use the entire body to contribute to a projection or movement. Segmentation, or separate body parts moving unconnected to each other, is seen in many Japanese, Korean and Okinawan Martial arts. Even in grappling arts you can see segmentation. That just means that the power is broken or not taking full advantage of the whole body.

It should be clearly understood that segmented motion can still be quite powerful.

> **One strong arm could knock a lot of people out. But the focus in Walu is to understand what relaxed power is all about and to learn how to move in numerous ways with the whole body reinforced with connected movement.**

Walu exercise movements were practiced faster than Tai Chi or Pakua, and it was attractive to a lot of students since the exercises were repeated for at least five minutes. This repetitiveness made it easy for a student to study and begin to feel the difference between segmentation and unitary movement. It is also a great exercise that allows a teacher to discover the issues in the body necessary to create unitary movement. The teacher can make small adjustments to make the person's efficiency and unitary action more precise. So it was a great bridge for those who were coming from segmented martial arts to internal martial arts. That is why it is referred to as a "Bridge Art."

Walu Symbol used by CBII practitioners.

One reason Walu is attractive is because many people are greatly attracted to power. When one learns to relax in the right way, they can quickly feel through apparatus training that their power has increased and in a different way. They don't try to tense up but develop a body state that can transfer the unitary movement and force to go through the body into the target. We often say the arts fall into two categories in projection and attacking. One category is like a hammer. The hammer is a powerful tool that pounds. The other category says that the body is a conduit. So one moves in a way that doesn't hammer in a segmented way but lets the energy send or whip the force out of the body, projecting into a target. This is the key ingredient in the study of Walu.

When learning the Walu, one usually has to swing the pendulum to the "too relaxed" side of study concerning the body state (tension) or "Peng." In this mode you don't hit objects as much but totally relax, making sure that your arm movement is caused by the dan dian and connection to the ground through the legs. You must create the arm movement through the movement of your legs, dan dian, and waist all working together. After one learns to be and move in this way, the body state must be increased in its muscle firmness. The key is to increase the body state without losing flexibility and relaxation. The added firmness is regulated evenly throughout the muscles rather than in one area. For one to maintain the conduit idea, one has to avoid the gripping and stiffness that is often used in a segmented method.

The rest of the Walu curriculum includes two forms and about 100 fighting techniques, which are divided into 3 sections. The sections were named General Self Defense, Dog Boxing and Master Text. Casey always said that these techniques are just well known techniques from many styles of martial art. He said that without the Walu energy, they are not special.

Beyond the movement and unitary method, Walu includes the "slide" that connects your body to the opponent's during the encounter so that one will get the opportunity to deliver the force with a hit or action. This very much compares to the forward pressure area of the Chinese Boxing encounter. I will speak of the Walu principles in another book, but this overview will give one the idea of its uniqueness.

The forms are unique in that they remind you of many styles mixed together. You will see elements of Pakua, Kempo, etc. It has a big variety of footwork, working spins and transitions through twisted stances that are in some cases very difficult, particularly for the beginner.

What Walu lacks in its curriculum is an organization of the basics, such as defenses and footwork in particular. It lacks an official dueling. Casey, at one point, challenged one of our students to try and make duels from the exercises and the five energy fist of Hsing-i.

This is not in the curriculum but is left up to the individual practitioner to add these things in. I have done this with various Walu curricula through the years.

So we can say that like Kempo, Walu needs a better basics formation in the curriculum. Kempo gives technique, Walu gives unitary execution of the technique, and internal arts teach the glue to put these things into an encounter.

Walu can often be helpful to Tai Chi people who do not feel the whole body connecting in Tai Chi. The concept of solo exercises is not new. They have been used in many arts. They are sort of like clay on a potters wheel. The student moves continually in a cycle, and the master can make gradual adjustments in the moment to fine-tune the student's movement and posture to a final product.

CHAPTER 11
WALLY JAY

WALLY JAY WAS like a father to Mr. Casey. He met him early on in the Jujitsu world that Casey was involved with in California and Hawaii.

> **Wally was unique. He had the Bruce Lee synthesis mind and found a way to make his jujitsu work better through smooth transitions and smaller circles. Small circle was not anything new, but was in great contrast to the Jujitsu that Wally had studied.**

Wally was initially on our CBII Board of directors but was pressured by the people who had ranked him and had him on a worldwide circuit to promote jujitsu. CBII was advertising him as a chin na teacher, and the people that gave Wally his living were offended since the chin na was a reference to the Chinese. This, of course, is what politics can do, as we see today in many areas. Cancel culture is not new.

Wally was just a wonderful person to be around. He was a great storyteller and told stories about Bruce Lee. He had a rich life and was always entertaining.

Wally taught at a couple of our Camps in Tennessee. He has some of the smoothest transitions in demonstrating his continuous chin na technique. He moved from one lock to the next if his opponent was escaping. It was as smooth as I have seen anyone do. This is not unlike what we are supposed to do in the execution of our Crown Eagle form. While our chin na coach Buddy Benford has his own method of execution, he had a lot of respect for Wally and gained from his training with him.

Professor Wally Jay

CHAPTER 12
TAKI KUMURA

TAKI KUMURA WAS PRETTY close to Bruce Lee's first student. He was Japanese and was very impressed that Bruce Lee showed him respect. Many Japanese Americans had suffered much disrespect during and after the war, and the Chinese also have a history with the Japanese. Taki mentioned that Bruce did not seem to have these biases, treating him with great respect and eventually becoming a very close friend.

Taki did not have any martial art background prior to Bruce Lee, and he was also around 40 or so when he began study. He learned a lot of the early JKD that Bruce taught. He told me that Bruce put a large focus on conditioning because he believed you must be in great shape to fight. So Taki was very disciplined and worked with Bruce in the early years when Bruce was in Seattle.

Bruce went on to work with Dan Inosanto and then became heavily involved in his Hollywood and Hong Kong movies. He kept in close touch with Taki all through those years.

My teacher, Mr. Casey, had a job in Seattle for two years before working in Germany. During those two years, he wanted to learn what Bruce Lee did early on in his training, so he went to Taki and studied with him. When Taki came to realize how talented and skilled Mr. Casey was, he did not understand why he had come to him. Taki told me that Mr. Casey showed him complete respect and learned his curriculum step by step as a beginner would have done.

Taki owned a couple of grocery stores. When I got to go to Seattle, it was after Mr. Casey had passed away. I had Taki's phone number, so I called him. As soon as I told him I was Mr. Casey's student, he asked me to come over to his office. He greeted me very kindly, and we talked for a while. He then decided to take me on a tour and went to show me Bruce Lee's gravesite. He was most kind. He invited me to come to his class in the evening, so I went over to watch.

The class was about an hour and a half. He spent the first hour on calisthenics that involved jogging in place, dropping to do push ups and doing core work in which he would hold both legs up and move them back and forth while lying on his back. It was nonstop and pretty taxing. Taki was 66 at the time, and he led the exercises with lots of energy. He probably had 50 people or so at the class, which was held in the basement of his grocery store. He finished the exercise portion in better condition than those in the class and breathing more calmly. He had lots of equipment, and his wall was full of pictures of his history with Bruce. Several books were there as well.

After an hour, he divided the class into several groups. He taught several of the teenage kids. He also had an old timers group that mostly worked on their own as well as a few more groups. His son and a couple other instructors led each group, doing things from the basics of Jeet Kune Do. After watching him the first hour, I was glad I didn't decide to participate. It was quite a workout. During the last half hour, he came over and talked to me more about his son and his students and more about Bruce. He told me that he only taught basics, and when a student learned everything well, he would recommend that they go to Dan Inosanto for advanced training. Afterward, he asked to buy a copy of my Synthesis Book. I just gave him one, and he gave it to his son and demanded that he read it. He was simply very nice, and it was a pleasure to meet him.

He told me that his mission was to work with a bunch of the younger teens who had various bouts with drugs or trouble in school. He worked with them not only on the martial arts and exercises, but also helped them with their everyday life. There were about 20 of them in his class that evening. He told me that was what kept him teaching. It also kept him in phenomenal shape. When I was younger, I had a poor impression of Bruce Lee. I thought he was arrogant and disrespectful to the older traditional generation of martial art teachers. After meeting Taki and also learning about how nice Dan Inosanto was, I thought a little more deeply about Bruce Lee, because bad people don't normally bring very nice quality guys into their inner circle. I began to read his notes more seriously.

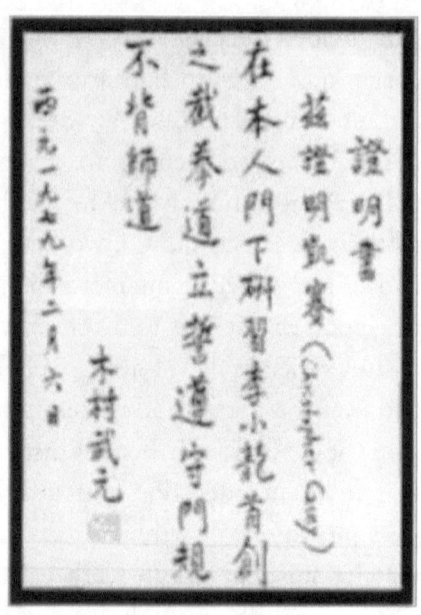

Mr. Casey's JKD Instructors Certificate

Mr. Casey asked me if I wanted to be certified in JKD. I told him I didn't mind learning the curriculum, but that I was dedicated to his Kai Sai Kung Fu. I told him that years earlier when Bruce Lee got popular, people came into my studio who wanted to learn JKD. Most were not serious but were just crazy about the Bruce Lee movies and what they saw in these movies.

I realize there are a lot of serious JKD people today and probably then, but at the time I didn't want to go that route. However, he did teach me the curriculum. JKD has a similar martial philosophy to Kai Sai Kung Fu. Most of the principles are there. One prominent one that is not there is rooting. It was always an interesting topic. Bruce said that rooting slowed him down. He obviously had much success with his gifted speed, etc. I am not convinced that rooting has to slow you down. Yes it could, but it actually helps you stay more stable with less chance of overextending. I understand his argument. It does speak to the fact that our individual bodies and talents will affect our martial arts in different ways.

Chinese Boxing is based on a set of principles that people of diverse sizes and talents can be under one flag, but have the flexibility to do the things that are the highest percentage for their success.

CHAPTER 13
DAN INOSANTO AND JEET KUNE DO

I NEVER MET DAN INOSANTO. There were a couple of opportunities that looked like I would, but they didn't work out. Several of my students have met him. Alan Baker is actually an instructor in JKD under Dan.

I have always heard positive things about him, and he seems to be humble as well. He has lived to an advanced age while staying in great shape.

Casey went to Dan and visited him a couple of times and spent some time on the phone with him as well. Dan and Taki were trying to form and organize the JKD group at the time. Casey had legal expertise, so they actually got him to draw up legal papers for organizing the JKD. In the end, the project was not pursued, and many of you know and are aware of how the history of using the JKD label has turned out.

Casey had some interaction with Dan and worked out with him, sharing ideas with one another. They did some Chi Sao together, and Dan demonstrated his Kali stick work for him. Casey told me once that if I ever wanted to learn how to move the Philippine sticks, I should go to Dan.

According to some of my students who have talked to Dan, he was highly complimentary when asked about Mr. Casey. In the pic below, you can see the nice note from Dan to Mr. Casey from earlier times.

J - Sifu Lo Man Kam with Master Dan Inosanto

Note from Dan Inosanto to Mr. Christopher Casey

CHAPTER 14
WING CHUN

Casey once said to me that Wing Chun may not be the best art, but there is none better that is built on simplicity.

FOR THOSE OF us who have committed to the Synthesis of Chinese Boxing, Wing Chun *represents* the principle of efficiency. So if one is doing any kind of technique in any aspect of the Synthesis, the question is always asked: Are we taking the most efficient and practical route with this technique? Even in the large circles of Pakua, once in touch with an opponent, there must be efficiency in the touch or one will waste energy and possibly give opportunity to the opponent.

Casey studied Wing Chun from several sources, but his main one was, of course, Lo Man Kam, the nephew of Yip Man. Wing Chun has been very popular in various parts of the world, including England and Germany. In some places it has lost a lot of followers due to the MMA, which has adjusted many students' attitudes to many martial arts. Wing Chun may have been more of a rare art had it not been for the fame of Bruce Lee, who had studied it from Yip Man. Because of his own references to the art, it became popular and was followed by many people. Interestingly, the one that made it famous used very little of the style; however, he held to the principle of efficiency in everything, as we do in the Chinese Boxing.

Early on when Casey learned from Lo Man Kam, everything was a big secret, which drew from some of the traditional views and ways of Chinese Martial Art. After many years, Casey talked Master Lo into putting the complete curricula of the style on film. There was, however, a warning that parts of the film could not be shown to anyone outside of Casey's inner circle. Our group tried to respect that for a long time, and I still do, keeping it to my students in my online Academy.

As time went on, every aspect of the Wing Chun curricula became public, as more and more groups and numbers began to promote the art. It became quite commercial to many.

The problem in many arts, Wing Chun being one of them, is that the original goals do not correspond with the actual training. In Chinese Boxing, we say that it is the sincere study of realistic martial arts. Not all people have this goal in their arts. Sometimes they give lip service to it, but you can recognize the difference through the balance of what they practice. In the case of Wing Chun, if the majority of the time one is doing Chi Sao, it is a small part of the big picture in realistic fighting. The point of touch and balance in the arms developed by Chi Sao could only be a moment in a fight. Either there is correct balance there or not. Fights can occur without any reference or need for this balance. Most people don't even do Chi Sao with forward pressure training. I realize some do, but it is a minority. When one does not include forward pressure, the options for finish are reduced, and there is less confidence in going from the close range of Chi Sao to the capture and finish. There is a touch involving the whole body on contact and not just the arms. So if the goal of our art is to study and be able to execute the Chinese Boxing realistic encounter, then the duels are important. But if that is all we do, we are not addressing many other critical areas.

In Chinese Boxing, we feel like Chi Sao is good for some arm touch; but in the encounter, you better also get an arm touch that deals with forward pressure during closing. Wing Chun can be taught this way, but my observation is that it is taught outside of the comprehensive idea, and the skills are often practiced out of balance to the big picture. I recognize this is only an opinion.

In the Kai Sai method of Wing Chun, the Mook Jong is very important training. First, it sharpens the angles of delivering technique after one learns the technique. It also plays a role in projection—not only developing the shock hit, but in learning to develop great power without crossing your center or central line. If one delivers power but misses the target because of an overextension of energy crossing the center, it makes one slow and unchangeable after the hit. Learning to hit independently of the target is a huge benefit of Mook Jong training.

You can see from our curriculum that Chinese Boxing does rely on several items in Wing Chun. Above the individual things, it is the principle of simplicity and efficiency that are the most important.

Lo's Wing Chun Emblem

Lo Man Kai holding Mr. Casey's Instructor Certificate

CHAPTER 15
LO MAN KAM

LO MAN KAM was the nephew of Yip Man. He followed Yip Man from Fatshan Province to the mainland to Hong Kong when the Japanese started coming through his province. He brought his nephew with him to Hong Kong and slowly developed his martial reputation there. He was a rich man and lost everything in his move to Hong Kong.

Lo eventually went to Taiwan to represent Yip Man in the more traditional culture. Yip Man wanted to move there, but was unable to do so.

Casey had an interest in Wing Chun, so when he started to travel to Taiwan, he sought out the best representative of Wing Chun.

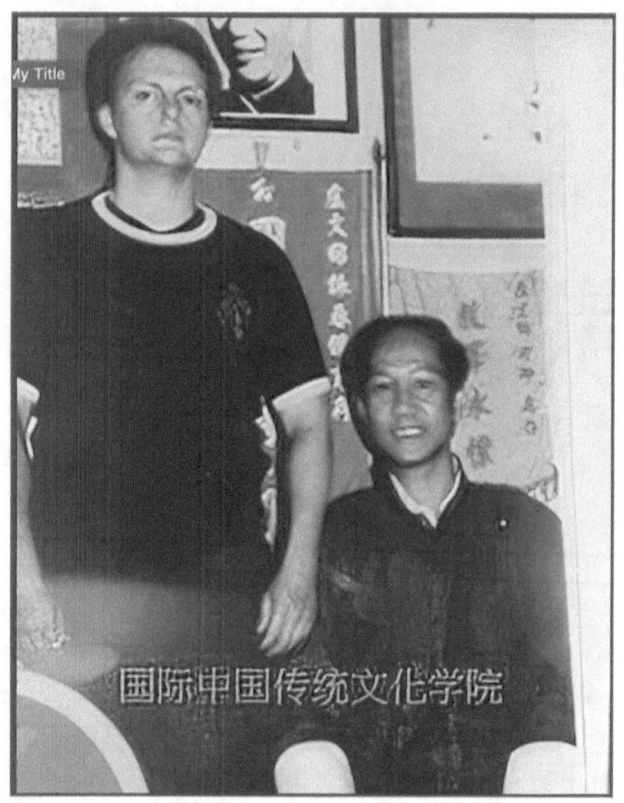

Lo was quite a character. He could speak three or four languages. Casey called him the physicist of Wing Chun. He would get out a protractor to fix Casey's angles on a Bong Sao. He was very exact in his teaching.

Casey spent a lot of time with Lo and became close to him. Lo was pretty traditional in the early days. He was willing to put his art on film for Casey, but he had to promise to limit who could get it. He was strict about not performing the Mook form or Bil Jee or the butterfly knives in public.

Casey was the first Caucasian to get a full teaching license from Lo.

Lo asked Casey to do the *Bai Shifu* ceremony with him. So Master Lo was the first to *Bai Shifu* Mr. Casey into his family clan.

He was quite loyal to Lo.

Lo is still alive and getting quite old. One of our CBII guys, Anthony Caucci, spent some time living in his house and studying in his classes. Lo was in great shape. He is very tiny. He had great lines and proverbs when teaching—kind of like what you would expect a great master to be able to say.

At one point, Lo's son came over to the USA, and one of my students in Chattanooga set him up for a weekend seminar. He found him to be very good but also detected some things that were different from our Chinese Boxing. It seems that Lo was not fond of rooting. Lo also had an extreme tucked in hip position. I think it appears to be a very locked position.

So while I may differ from Lo on some things, I still have great respect for him as my teacher's teacher and a great teacher of Wing Chun Gong Fu.

Lo Man Kam and the Butterfly Knives

CHAPTER 16
PAKUA

RIGHT BEFORE CASEY came back to the states from Germany, he told me that as he moved into the next few years, he was ready to reveal his Chinese Boxing and also wanted to teach Hsing-i to Manfred and Pakua to me. These were arts he had practiced for several years to develop his internal skills. He was personally planning to spend more time in developing his Tai Chi, and he wanted to make sure that these other two arts were preserved. He felt the internals could produce something necessary in training the body and body state.

Manfred never really studied from Casey again after 1981 or so. He did visit Casey for a week toward the end of Casey's life. Manfred had learned a little bit of Hsing-i but never got the chance to get corrected by Casey.

When I began training in Stanford, Casey focused on Pakua as my main art. We were doing other things as well, but as far as the art he wanted me to train for my body, it was Pakua. He had wanted to work with Manfred on Hsing-i because Manfred had more of a linear way of fighting, and Hsing-I was very linear. He wanted me to do the Pakua because he felt my strength was in my lateral movement. To him, Tai Chi was the most difficult art. He did end up working with me on Tao's Tai Chi and his version of Hsing-i Chuan.

The Pakua was his version, so we have called it Kai Sai Pakua Chang. He also referred to it as Pakua Celestial Dragon Eight Direction Boxing. It was a synthesis no doubt, but it was something that Wang Shu Shen taught that was unique. Wang mostly taught a couple of shorter forms to most everyone that we have seen who claim his tutelage or lineage. Casey told Wang that he was looking to learn a martial Pakua, so Wang said he would have to take private classes.

The form was very different. It integrated 8 Palm Changes with 8 Animals into a form that would last for about an hour. If you did the principles and remained rooted, it was a beast to practice. His idea of staying down in a root for an extended period of time was one of the major benefits and battles. I asked a student once who had learned the Pakua form to do the first two animals with changes in the form and not come out of his root. This student knew how to root. He quit when he hit the second animal first change (about 5-7 minutes). He not only quit, he decided to quit Pakua because he said that it would be too hard to accomplish. While I thought that was an overreaction to what had happened, I appreciated the fact that he understood what the goal was. He just sought an easier solution.

Even though a Chinese Boxing Encounter may only last a short time, one must have the automation to root and stay down with the energy most of the time. Could this be accomplished without practicing an hour form? Probably, but certainly the lengthy exercise staying down in the legs would tend to burn the *rooting sensation* into the body. This is the art where I learned how to root. Almost anyone can be taught to root standing in place with a little but of prompting, but to move in a root and eventually fight in a root is very difficult.

Pakua has the most natural stepping footwork of all the arts, and the turns and twists make it the most versatile in footwork. The walking in Pakua is the closest thing to the advance step in our Chinese Boxing Encounter. Tai Chi builds great stance and structure and flow. Its stepping transitions are not usually practiced in a continually centered method like the walk in Pakua. So the transition from good structure to walking with good structure is one of the greatest contributions of Pakua. None of the internal form practice means that you can fight. They are only training methods that develop body movement with the principles that one wants to build deep into the body so that they are automatic habits when one fights. This is what makes Pakua unique.

Mr. Casey practiced Pakua for eight years—five years very intensely. So when Casey came back from Germany, the art of Pakua was my prime focus for the next several years. Pakua takes a lot of effort and work to develop. I was learning it mechanically, but it took some time before I implemented the internal principles. This is the art that taught me to root. When you spend so much time continuously moving your body, the excess tension eventually lets go, and you begin to relax into your legs. Of course, you need corrections as you go, but the sheer magnitude of the time spent in the form leads you in the direction of rooting.

Pakua looks so strange, one wonders how it could possibly be a practical martial art. Of course, Casey had the answer to all this. The looks are deceiving, and all of our arts become efficient when understood and when the application is applied to the Chinese Boxing Encounter. One normally does not discover the efficiency without the practice of touch that is provided in the duels of the internal arts.

When I practiced practical combat, it didn't feel anything like when I was practicing Pakua. But with time, things happen when you have a great art to practice; and the root, unitary movement and other things begin to appear in the moment.

One thing Pakua did was increase my balance and changeability. I believe that is due to its unique footwork and, in particular, the circle walk and spinning. It builds in a balance even though you may not realize it in the beginning. After several years, I started to notice it. So the exercise does have an effect on your total equilibrium.

The other thing very special about Pakua is that it is the best link from a traditional art to the unique art of Chinese Boxing.

One of the unique things about Chinese Boxing is that in the Encounter, you develop an attack or counterattack that moves very fast with forward pressure, using the skills of yielding to move around obstacles in order to capture the opponent body to body. No other art tries to make this type of transition in this way.

Others come close, but the footwork of Hsing-i and Tai Chi aren't quite as good at making this transition. Of course, you can get there in either one and even in non-internal arts, but Pakua is the best because of the walking. All the principles of rooting and unitary body state must transfer from posture to a continual walk. This is one of the hardest things to get in Chinese Boxing.

The art is not for everyone. If you have equilibrium issues, then spinning and circling may not sit well with you. If you have past injuries or bad knees, etc., one may have trouble with the changing, twisting, turning and spinning actions. So it is not for everyone, and that is partially why it is so rare. It is no where near as popular as Tai Chi.

The structural things I mentioned that were so important that I was introduced to in Chen Tai Chi were transferred to my Pakua practice over time. It certainly gave it a new look and feel and was much smarter as well as better for my body.

Even today, I have very few students working on Pakua. Maybe because the age group of most of my students is older, and Pakua is more difficult physically than Tai Chi or Hsing-i. It is still very special and unique in its training and movement.

Pakua Posture in the Seventh Change

CHAPTER 17
WANG SHU SHEN

WANG SHU SHEN was certainly one of a kind. The man was larger than life both physically and mentally. He had some physical infirmities and was often made fun of because of his size. No one probably did that to his face. He is one of the legends that was said to have never been defeated in combat. Some of the younger clips of Wang Shu Shen show how his mastery of Pakua was evident. He made this strange mysterious art look scary. The speed he had for his size was very impressive.

Wang was another casualty of the Communist takeover in China. Records seem to show that he was a priest for an unusual religion in China called I-quan. Some say he was known more for this than the Pakua. This religion was actually a synthesis of all religions. Some of his followers provided a way for him to escape to Taiwan. He was under a watch in China anyway, because a religion such as this was not liked or trusted by the government. The Communist would have had little tolerance.

Wang is difficult to trace in history. A lot of Chinese are hard to trace since they had one name when they were younger and then got a second name later on. Writings reveal that his lineage was a little difficult to trace, but his skill was highly recognized. He was also a synthesizer in his martial arts as well as his religion. He taught Tai C'hi, Pakua and Hsing-i. His strength was Pakua, but the first video I ever saw of him was of Hsing-i. He was older and leading a group of men through the elements. When one watches this, one would normally not be impressed.

Master Wang Shu Shen and Mr. Casey

I later saw younger clips of him doing his Pakua which would be quite impressive to anyone's eye. Wang teamed with another famous master in Taiwan to put together a Tai Chi style. It looks somewhat like Yang style. He stated that he interspersed some Chen Tai Chi into this new style. I saw some footage of Wang doing a push hands rotation with a student which was definitely Chen method. So he did have some kind of exposure to Chen Style. Other clips show him doing a rotation with double swords.

Casey's experience with Wang was unique. He studied privately with the help of a translator. Wang was not in great health in those days and would often sit while his student taught the movement to

Mr. Casey. When the student was doing application, Casey was not easily impressed, so Wang would get out of his chair and show the application to and on Mr. Casey, which definitely impressed him.

Casey developed a good relationship with Wang. Toward the end of his life, he gave Casey a set of several hundred large photographs that he had made for documenting his Pakua book. Casey showed me a low resolution copy of these photos; but when Casey died, I was unable to get a look at these photos since Mrs. Casey stored things away.

Wang had financial issues and worked in Japan several years where a doctor took care of him. This Doctor was also a Japanese style empty hand master. So Wang would share his art of Pakua and teach at his school.

Casey never taught me Pakua weapons. The only weapon he talked about was the deer horn knives. Wang would buy a thousand cheap samurai swords and use the deer horn knives to practice blocking and twisting the blade away from the opponent.

One story by Robert Smith sort of belittled Wang, saying he was not as good as Cheng Man Ching; but my teacher had a very different opinion of this situation. We will never know, but it is still great to think about the rich history CBII was able to tap into.

Pakua Grandmaster Wang Shu Shen

CHAPTER 18
HSING-I

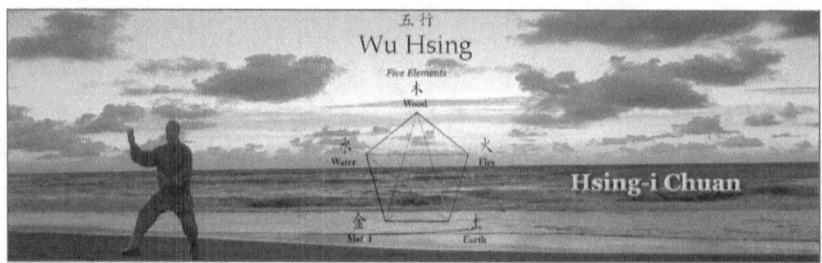

DURING THE BEST years with Mr. Casey, he spent some time with me teaching the Hsing-i curriculum. He had a great love for this art. It was something like the internal version of Wing Chun, being very direct and practical in the movements.

We train the five elements as the core of the training. The system also involves practicing small combinations, representing 20 animals. Of course, that is not traditional, as there are usually 10 or 12 animals associated with Muslim and non-Muslim Hsing-i methods.

Mr. Casey looked at the five elements as projections. The projection of dropping force, rising force, straight force, zigzag projection and circular energy.

He kept the focus on this, and the animals were not emphasized very much in his teaching. He told me that each animal he taught, which was a short combination (2-6 movements), also had a long form associated with it. He said he documented all these forms but barely practiced them. He was focused on the five projections.

Casey worked with me the majority of the time on the element Metal. He taught the essence of each element and the changes between them that are desirable for both offense and defense. He also spent some time on the idea of the duels. He said that dueling was dangerous because you could not apply the projection at full power at close range safely. So he normally worked on the positions that one needed to *get to*, in order to apply the energy. Entry to the position was studied as well.

Casey encouraged us to combine some of the Hsing-i energies with some of the Walu energies. He even wanted us to make some duels from this combination. Jeff Holler did the most work in this area.

In summary, the important things I learned from Hsing-i were the efficient 5 projections. The other thing was the understanding that

when applying a projection one should go deep into the target

and not just a couple of inches. So in applying the crash down of Metal, it was not to occur on the arms or surface of the head. But one would move deep, and the exit point during the crash might be at the elbow or closer, and the steps would end up very deep to have the balance necessary under the projection. This idea of depth was taken into the application of all styles and methods in Chinese Boxing.

CHAPTER 19
SHEN MOU HAI

Mr. Casey and Shen Mou Hai

SHEN MOU HAI was a master of many talents. His family art was Black Shantung Tiger. It has a number of kicks in it that are very unique. Off-center kicks are done frequently in the Shantung Forms.

Shen was a master of Chin na and demonstrated very powerfully on his students. Mr. Casey always had brutal chin na, and Shen is the closest to this that I have seen of Casey's teachers.

Shen taught Casey some Tai Chi. Casey referred to it as the Grand Tai Chi. It was more like the Long Yang Style, but Shen's characteristic of the bobbing head comes from Black Shantung Tiger. These head actions were evident in all of his internal arts. Shen only taught Tai Chi publicly. It was privately that Casey tapped into his Crown Eagle and Shuai Chaio, as well as his three internal arts.

I had a student who's brother studied with Shen Mou Hai in Taiwan. He studied the Tai Chi and had no idea that Shen could teach all these other things. He wondered how Casey got this to happen. It was probably no more complicated than that he paid his teachers well. He also practiced hard and did not embarrass his teachers in any way publicly or cause them to lose trust in him.

He spent the most time with Master Shen on Hsing-i. He believed Shen was best and most accomplished in this art. He thought Shen could do some remarkable things. There was one apparatus in which Shen could lift 300 pounds with a machine called a Metal Drop Machine. Your arm was strapped to a rope and cable which was connected to weights on the ground. When one was doing the element Metal, one would drop the hand and body which would lift the weights. Most of us struggled with thirty pounds in this exercise. I saw Casey do 90 lbs but never saw Shen do it.

It was very expensive to take lessons from Shen. He told Casey that he could teach him anything and that he would not need any other teacher. Casey had a lot of respect for his martial art skill, but preferred to study with a teacher because of their specialty. He was considered one of Casey's main teachers, but the time he spent with him was less than Master Tao and Master Lo Man Kam.

Shen Mou Hai's Calligraphy and Artistry

CHAPTER 20
MANFRED STEINER

MANFRED STEINER came into my journey while Casey was in Germany. Casey had just started me with the Chinese Boxing idea before moving to Germany for a year. I saw Casey three times that year when he returned to Atlanta to see his family.

Manfred Steiner

During that year, he began to talk to me about Manfred. Manfred and I were the only students of Casey that were taught for a significant amount of time. Manfred's was short, just a little over a year, but it was intense and frequent.

Casey started looking around when he moved to Germany. He went by several schools to see what people were practicing. At one school he ran into Manfred. They talked for a while and made a quick connection. Manfred was interested in philosophy and serious martial arts, so they knew they had things in common. Casey needed to have people to practice with, and he asked Manfred if he wanted to come over and see some films of some of his teachers. Manfred went to Casey's house and looked at the films.

Afterward, Mr. Casey asked him if he saw anything he liked.

Manfred concurred, and Casey asked him if he wanted to start training in any of these things. So that was the start of it. Manfred had a strong mind and an unbelievable physical presence. He had won a Judo Championship in Germany and was the Kyokushinkai Karate Champion of Europe. He had advanced power, strength, speed and athletic ability. Casey had developed his Chinese Boxing Synthesis to a high degree, and I think Manfred was the ultimate partner or opponent for Casey to test his ideas and skills.

Manfred was game and willing to endure the punishment. When I studied with Casey, I did not want to turn things into a competition. I was afraid that would either get me hurt or would hinder my student status with Mr. Casey. Manfred resisted and competed at times; and when he did, he got injured. He would come back for more training over and over again even with the injuries. Although injured, he was at Mr. Casey's place five or six days a week for that one year. Casey would tell Manfred that he thought his shoulder had been injured or dislocated; and Manfred would say, "Yes, but I have another shoulder that works."

So Casey would tell me these stories. He also kept telling me that he wanted to see Manfred duel and spar with me. I told Casey that I did not have a big desire to compete with such a dominant force. Casey then gave me a lecture in which he said that all of life is a competition, and you have to learn to conquer it. So Casey arranged for Manfred to come visit me in 1981. When I saw Manfred move as he taught our group and worked with me privately, I realized that Casey had not exaggerated his talents. Manfred worked with me and would train rough, but he showed me a lot of respect and really tried to teach. I think Casey may have threatened him not to injure me.

At that point in time, I did not think there was a prayer that I could ever be competitive with Manfred. When Mr. Casey moved back to the states the next year, it was a good time for me. The next few years were the best time I had learning from Casey. He told me at the time that he could control Manfred and that he could teach me to do the same thing. I doubted, but I will say that he taught me a lot, and I began to develop the principles of Chinese Boxing. Manfred came back to visit a couple of years later; and when we worked together, I felt that I was not in same place I had been before. I felt much more confident because Casey had taught me with this goal in mind.

When Casey died, Manfred was really depressed, as we all were, and he kind of dropped out of martial art temporarily. He had worked for the government for many years as an artist, drawing maps. After Casey's death, he quit his job and went into the healing arts. That was quite a shock to many people. He treated animals with acupuncture and chiropractic technique. He came over to Arizona to learn this from a chiropractor. Although he returned to his martial arts, he quit teaching all his students that he had taught in the past. I don't think his students ever understood that. Later he seemed to get another small group of students. He believed he understood Casey's ideas and said he always used them. He did go into other martial arts to learn and study. Manfred passed away a few years ago after an illness.

His students had found me after he quit, and I ended up going to Germany with my student Rick Lupe four times over a decade or so. Detlef Zimmermann was the head of Manfred's old school, and there were a couple other seniors that we met and had a wonderful time. Each time I was there, they contacted Manfred to ask if he wanted to come to a meal. So each time I went to Germany, we were able to get together for some catching up. The first trip was the most memorable.

Manfred also had a strong effect on several of my students. If Manfred did not know Chinese Boxing, he would still be a great force and difficult to fight against. With the Chinese Boxing, it made him very special. Manfred, Casey and I all were different and had different skills. Manfred, being so strong, did not have to develop as much yielding skill to deal with most people. So, he could yield but didn't need to against most fighters. The reason is that most fighters do not yield well, and Manfred's power would overcome. Casey's skill was with his mind hit technique and his great projection and penetration once he got a hold of you. His projection skills were awesome. I do not have near the projection skills of Casey or the strength of Manfred, so my focus has been on my footwork to allow me to yield and position myself at angles that would allow me to be successful by avoiding force.

Those that study energy boxing can be in agreement as to the theory and the encounter method, yet be quite different in certain areas. One must learn to maximize strengths and hide the weaknesses as much as possible.

We miss Manfred, as do his students in Germany. He definitely had an effect on my perspective of Chinese Boxing.

James Cravens and Manfred Steiner

CHAPTER 21
1981 - CBII AND INDOOR STUDENT

WHEN CASEY RETURNED to the States around the end of 1981, I began some intensive training with him every three months. I stayed with him up to a week each time. The sessions were intense and covered so much material that I would leave in a fog. I had to learn how to take notes while learning from such an eccentric personality.

Mr. Casey did not particularly like people or to be around them. The one exception was his wife Vickie. That was a match that was unique and did not interfere with his lonely private being.

I probably studied with Casey more than anyone else over a longer period of time, but it was still hard to be with him more than a few days. It was even harder for him, as he just didn't like people that much.

As I mentioned earlier, he was condescending and spoke with a vocabulary that was very difficult to follow because of his knowledge of the English language. But after a while, things changed a bit, and he became much more engaging and nicer to me. The last few years he even conceded to try and record portions of his art on video. He even developed so that in his last years, he felt a need to do more to make sure I was able to understand and teach his art. Not long after we began training in Stanford, he wanted to do a *Bai Sifu* picture and make me an indoor student. At that time, he gave me a certificate which indicated my accomplishment, and he gave me a title of Professor because of my interest in learning the detail of the art.

I was not comfortable with the title, so I have never asked my students to use it. When I moved to Florida initially, the person I went into business with was a marketing guy, so he had his whole school call me Professor. When I was back in Tennessee and some of the Florida guys were around, they wondered what in the world was going on with the title. Casey was pretty low on ceremony and titles. After all, he had learned his martial arts by going beyond the need for titles. He had earned his share, but his greatest education came after all the titles had been accomplished when he learned from genuine energy boxers.

Indoor student is just a designation, but everyone must own their art—not just the trimmings, but actually know the art intimately from training.

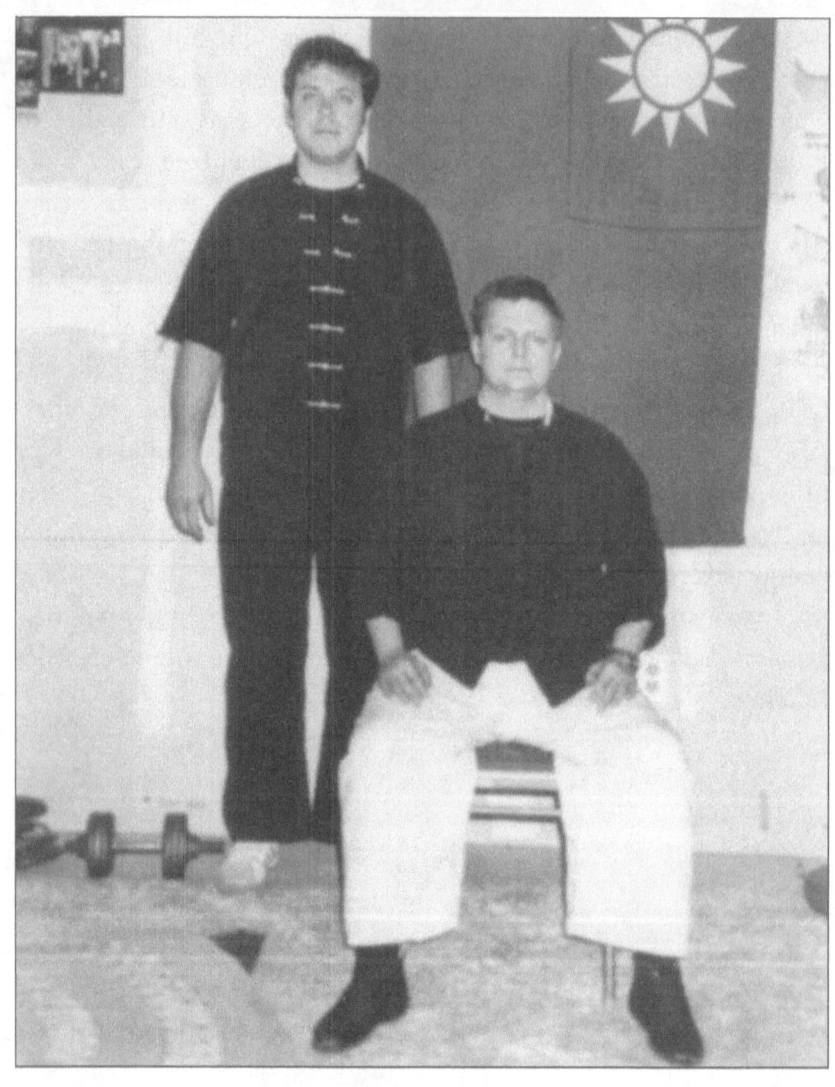

Bai Shifu James Cravens and Christopher Casey

CHAPTER 22
CHINESE BOXING SYNTHESIS

1981 WAS when Casey put together the curriculum he called Kai Sai Kung Fu. It had about ten Boards. The Boards idea came from Henry Okazaki's Kodakan Jujitsu School in Hawaii. He actually had his curricula up on wooden boards in the school, divided by category. So Casey used the idea. He did not make this curriculum for a progressive study, but it was laid out simply by his favorite things in each category, such as hands, kicks, blocks or defenders, footwork, chin na, shuai chaio, collision or self-defense, etc.

He modified it a little, but we did practice it for a while. The boards and synthesis evolved in different forms. After moving to Florida, I wanted to preserve everything I had learned from Casey; so I set up a Synthesis curriculum that had 16 boards that included a lot of things on many of the boards. It was a little over the top. After teaching it for a couple of years, I realized I needed something a bit more compact. So I developed the Boards with 16 categories with only 12 items on each board. This was the main CB curriculum we used for a long time. It was the Chinese Boxing Core Synthesis.

There was a period that I wanted to go smaller and have three things on each board and call it Core of the Core. This was more of an analytical exercise in which students had to examine the three things I had chosen and decide if they thought these were the bottom line core things that were needed in each category.

In the past couple of years with the creation of the Chinese Boxing Instructors Association, I have gone back to a longer curriculum for instructors. Nothing important has really changed, as the principles and the study of the Encounter is still the focus.

Synthesis must be trained so that it has the same utility of a pure style. There may not be such a thing as a pure style because almost every founder of an art drew from various sources, making every pure style a type of Synthesis. A pure style normally has few options to respond to different things. With fewer options the odds increase in developing better instincts for fighting assuming the options are excellent.

When one can simplify an art, there is a better chance that a person can develop if he has fewer options that make up his choices of responses and instincts.

A Synthesis must do the same thing. The worst thing about JKD or CB Synthesis is when it is a bunch of things the person likes, but there is no connection and no priority for the instincts necessary to fulfill the idea and theory of the art.

So a synthesis is a difficult thing to put together. It is not just collecting a bunch of techniques. It has to be woven into an art form which is simple, but yet effective in developing the least amount of instincts to develop everything needed in combat. Without careful thought and practice, a synthesis could easily confuse the practitioner. It is like having a toolbox with many tools; it is difficult to find the right ones with any speed to get the job done. If the toolbox had less and carefully chosen tools that would accomplish the job, it would be far better. It is a bit more complex with a synthesis martial art, but the idea and challenges are the same.

The advantage is that one who develops a synthesis attempts to start with a blank page with no preconditions. We are so influenced by our past habits and techniques, we can miss what it takes to form a truly great synthesis.

So when we are working on the Boards, we should not be focused on the list of techniques, but on whether a technique fits the philosophy of the art. Our boundaries are the study of realistic combat, desiring high percentage and high probability strategies and techniques that can reach maximum efficiency in getting the job done. Everything must fit within that philosophy.

Chinese Boxing Boards - Core Synthesis

Hand / Arm
1. Whiphand
2. Fore Fist
3. Spadehand
4. Pendulum Palm
5. Wing Arm
6. Reverse Punch
7. Lift Punch
8. Bolo
9. Monkey Overhead
10. Fist Drop
11. Palm Methods (4)
12. Short Range Punch

Foot / Leg
1. Lift
2. Side
3. Shuffle A Front
4. Instep Reverse
5. Shuffle A Round
6. Side
7. Shuffle B Round
8. Torque
9. Round
10. Front Stomp
11. Groin Scoop/Missile
12. Inside Sweep/Heel

Defenders
1. Chum
2. Pak
3. Lap
4. Bong
5. Jut
6. Condor
7. Man
8. X Taun Sao
9. X Guan Sao
10. Triangle
11. Knee
12. Separating Palm

Traversers
1. Shuffle A
2. Advance
3. Triangle
4. Shuffle B
5. Scampering
6. Nervous Feet
7. Drunken Step
8. Monkey Overstepping
9. JKD Shuffle Series
10. Offense
11. Yield and Counter
12. Stop Hit

Combinations
1. Chain Punching
2. Bil Jee
3. Figure 8 Up/Down
4. Whiphand/jabbing
5. Lead Hand Rear Hand
6. Switchblade
7. Forefist-Elbow or Hook
8. Spade-Lop-spade
9. Three Hand Monkey
10. Spade-Pak-Wingarm
11. Pak-check-Spade
12. Duck/Palm-check-spade

Unitary Exercises
1. Snake Cobra
2. Outer Circles
3. Sledgeing
4. Condor
5. Pakua Palm
6. Water Exercise
7. Teacup
8. Four Corners
9. Circle Within a Circle
10. Tiger
11. Four/Five Hand Blitz
12. Vortexing (3)

Projection
1. Pattern
2. Structure
3. Ground Leverage
4. Twisting Force - SR
5. Relaxation - Body State
6. Speed
7. Gravity - Sledging
8. Shock vs Thrust Force
9. Unitary
10. Exercises - Application, Sand training, Mook Jong Ex., EX and IN Hand training

Conditioning
1. Soft~Hard= Changeable
2. Strength ~ Power
3. Stamina ~ Endurance
4. Coordination - Agility
5. Warmup ~Core~Cool Down
6. Air
7. Apparatus
8. Partners
9. Postures
10. Internal systems
11. External parts

Chin na
1. Lop
2. Finger
3. Wrist (3)
4. Elbow (3)
5. Bracelet
6. Vising methods
7. Short Arm Scissors
8. Neck
9. Ambush
10. CE Section 1-2
11. CE Section 3-4
12. CE Section 5-6

Collision
1. Distance
2. First Response
3. Misc grabs
4. Elbow
5. Knee
6. Vital Points
7. Response to Angles
8. Three Strategies
9. SD against Weapons
10. Multiple Attack Strategy
11. Using the Environment
12. Finishing

Ground Fighting
1. Takedown Defense
2. Breakfalls(movtoGrDef)
3. Takedowns(MovtogrOff)
4. Top Position on Gr
5. Bottom Posiiton on Gr
6. Ground Movement
7. Submission Finishes
8. Strike Finishes on Gr
9. Kicks/Sweeps on Gr
10. Drills
11. Duels
12. Overall Strategy

Skill Drills
1. Hsieh Sao
2. Pushes
3. Reaction to Push
4. Non-telegraphic
5. Folding Skills
6. Triangle and Adv Step
7. Jeet Sao Exercises
8. Four Hand Monkey
9. Bong Sao/Lop Sao
10. Basic Arm/Body Balance
11. Single Chi Sao Rotation
12. Push Hands Rotations

Duels
1. Crossed Wrist
2. Standard Chin na Tie up
3. Single Hand Process *
4. Double Chi Sao *
5. Push Hands *
6. Pakua Joint Hands *
7. Hsing-I Joint Hands *
7. Kong Sao
8. Additional Duels
   A. Chi Tek, B. Fukien Joint Hands

Fighting Theory
1. Ten Principles
2. Chinese Boxing Encounter
3. Three EntryRequirements
4. Mechanical variations:
   A. Body placement - legs B. Body Placement-Hands, C. Closed vs Open
5. Speed
6. Distance and Timing
7. Touch
8. Mind Hit and Strategy

Mind Training
1. Mind in Combat:
   - Mind Hit Execution
   - Mind Hit Defense
   - Distraction
   - Intensity
   - Pain
   - Confidence
2. The Learning Mind
   Opening - Attitude
   Imaging
   Method of Judging success failure
3. Synthetic Apriori Fist
4. Drills

History/Philosophy
1. History of CBII
2. Yin Yang
3. Wu Hsing
4. I-Ching
5. History of: Shaolin, Taiji Chuan, Pakua Chang, Hsing-I Chuan, and Wing Chun
6. Differences in Western and Eastern Thought
7. Mind Hit Book by Casey

CHAPTER 23
SAS-G - CHING BAO GONG KA

SAS-G STANDS for Special Action Service - Group. Mr. Casey studied with Shen Mou Hai, and Shen was the teacher of the top bodyguards and special training of the secret police in Taiwan. They had a camp in which Casey actually participated. SAS-G is a practical, realistic art used in life and death situations.

The study in which Casey participated was the background for this SAS-G curriculum. He also referred to this curriculum as Jing Dao Gong Ka or "real boxing."

When I was learning the Chinese Boxing from Casey, I had a school in Chattanooga and was teaching kempo and Shaolin commercially, but was practicing Chinese Boxing with my advanced students. I began to feel frustrated since I had come to believe that Chinese Boxing was the best art. So why was I teaching other arts that had totally different theories of fighting?

Mr. Casey used to call me a lot during those years. About every other day, we would talk late at night. I was glad that we could do this because it allowed him to explain things that I had not yet integrated from our last training session. Many questions would come up, and being able to talk with him greatly helped me get over some of the problems I was having. Our conversations were an awesome education in his art.

He always asked me how my school was doing. I would complain to him about teaching the kempo and Shaolin, but believing in the Chinese Boxing. So the next thing I knew, he told me that when he was flying back from Germany, he had organized a curriculum that he thought might help me in teaching in the Commercial School and would prepare students for the Chinese Boxing.

He called it the SAS-G Gonka Real Boxing. He drew from what he had learned from Shen Mou Hai and other sources as well.

He felt that it would be of great interest to beginners and would give fundamental, useful, practical training. Before doing the SAS-G curriculum, he incorporated a few practical Wing Chun blocks that would protect one against most hand attacks. After teaching these basics from Wing Chun, we began the Four Parts to the SAS-G Curriculum.

The first part was empty hand. The second category comprised the knife techniques, and the third category consisted of the Cane or umbrella techniques. The final category was a study of hand projection into vital points followed by elbow strikes. This was derived from his Mind Hit technique.

There was keen interest in this curriculum. The problem that arose was that while the techniques were great, one had to be quite skilled on entry to do some of the things in the first three categories. In fact, Casey might have been one of the only ones who could be successful on entry to execute these techniques. Once in position on entry, the rest could usually be done by most everyone with some practice.

When I moved to Florida, the school that was bringing me there to teach had been focused on doing the SAS-G curriculum for about a year. As I watched the class, I was seeing that the entries were terrible, but the rest was okay.

So I spent some time organizing the curriculum into Beginners, Intermediate and Advanced sections. The advanced technique was what Casey had taught on the technique. The Beginning and Intermediate versions were easier entry setups. This made a lot more sense to me and was a more realistic study.

To give an example of the problem. When a person threw a punch, the response was catching the wrist and elbow in a chin na vice and going from there. Well, this is very difficult to do in a realistic situation with any consistency. Since Casey could do this, we just referred to this as the advanced version. If one was in close enough range to grapple and the opponent extended his arm, then the vice on that arm was much easier than catching a punch with a vice. The rest would follow.

The knife techniques were done with the person who was doing the technique, the one using the knife. Many of the knife techniques were more practical. The cane/umbrella was a bit more difficult to control. There were many good things in these techniques. It is more dangerous for partners working with these weapons, so more caution and control needs to be used to prevent injury.

In section four, the pain that is created by the vital point elbow study and the pain coming from the wooden cane techniques would cause people to feel a lot of pain very intensely. Strangely, many people think more of what they are learning when they experience some of this controlled pain.

This was primarily meant to entice an interest in learning for beginners. In the end, these stimuli wear out, and one actually needs to be very good at basics, such as footwork, etc. So you can see how it may have been useful commercially in the beginning compared to other curriculums.

Within the curriculum itself, there are lots of valuable things. When a technique is done well on an opponent in any art, it is valuable if it is accomplishing the goal of the art. The vital point elbow section has very valuable information that encompasses all of realistic fighting.

CHAPTER 24
ADAMANTINE BOXING

ADAMANTINE MEANS UNBREAKABLE. In the study of Chinese Boxing and the study of realistic fighting, we have said there are many challenges. It is difficult and dangerous to practice realist things on your partner. So one must be creative to find ways for training safely.

Mr. Casey set an example and came up with an idea one day that he called Adamantine Boxing. It was a sparring method/drill. Now most sparring methods have an idea in mind as to what one wants to work on that is necessary for the Chinese Boxing Encounter. This method was designed to focus on the number one target, the eyes, and the number two target, the groin. We purchased two sets of some very expensive equipment for sparring. It had an external groin protecter, along with shin protectors, thigh protectors, chest protector and a helmet with a plastic face guard. An option to the helmet was a good set of goggles. The competition did not involve a collection of points; the first hit to the vital ended the fight.

The match began in a crossed wrist position. The first one to get a clear hit on the groin or the eyes won the fight. The fight could be over instantly if the crossed wrist position was successful with an instant attack to the goggles. The fight would continue until someone hit the groin or eyes without a block.

Now you could paint a long list of reasons why this is not realistic, and you would be right. But then, it was just an exercise to draw everyone's attention to two things. 1) How good and efficient are you in hitting the number one and number two targets of the opponent? 2) How well do you defend against the attack to the groin and eyes? A little of this sparring reveals that we don't protect those two areas very well, and we are not all used to attacking these two vital targets. Many methods and competitions do not allow techniques to these targets, so one can actually be poorly trained in what appears to be a simple thing.

The purpose of the exercise is to improve a lot in these two areas. With practice, everyone was able to improve a good deal. Now when you do a specialized exercise that misses the mark in realistic fighting, you have to go back to drills that bring some other realism into the picture.

We must remember that balance must be developed in this difficult study of Chinese Boxing. Again, the purpose is to safely develop skill in striking the vitals while increasing awareness of protecting them. The groin is more difficult to hurt with a random strike in a fight, but a strike to the eyes can have great effect, even if all it does is draw a defender into a vulnerable position for a continued attack.

Adamantine Boxing is just a tool, and should be one of many exercises that round out the training in Chinese Boxing.

CHAPTER 25
CROWN EAGLE

CROWN EAGLE IS the name of a chin na form that Mr. Casey learned from the School of Grand Chaining in Taiwan. If you look at one of the older books written by Robert Smith called <u>Chinese Boxing: Masters and Methods</u>, you will see a photo of Shen Mou Hai when he was younger and learning in that school.

Mr. Casey was introduced to this school and made a friend with whom he could practice the form in Taiwan. The form was a monster, having 360 movements. In many chin na two-person forms, one person does a technique on the partner, who then counters with one of his own. This back and forth continued throughout the chin na form.

In Crown Eagle there are 36 sections that have around ten movements in each section. So one person does the ten movements. In the form, a lock or movement is applied, and the partner changes or escapes the movement; however, the person dong the techniques changes to another technique when the partner escapes. So in a sense, there is an offensive side for about ten movements, and then it reverses and changes to a defensive side for ten movements. When one person gets through the section with about ten moves, there is a transition of a couple of moves where the two partners change roles with offense changing to the defensive side etc.

One thing that is difficult but necessary is that when a lock is being applied, it is important that the partner reacts or resists so that the following technique makes sense. Without the proper reactions from a partner, the follow up technique would not be done. So two people have to work together, and that may take quite a bit of effort. The two people should go into the practice understanding this and trying to help each other. Of course, you can say that one is not training realistically, but reactions to chin na are many; and overall, the form is trying to give you good answers of what to do in various situations. More instinctive training is involved in some of the categories below.

The full curriculum in the school had five areas of study.

1. The form **Crown Eagle** - thirty six sections containing 360 movements.

2. **Lethal Locator** - In this area, the application of each move is studied so that if the technique works, one learns how to finish the fight.

3. **Death Messenger** - This area uses a nerve and vital point pressure attack in order to accelerate the finish of the fight.

4. **Ruler Ring** - In this area of study, a steel ring is placed over the arms of both partners while they do the form. This serves different purposes as it bounces around different parts of the arms. One must not respond to the pressures from this ring while doing the form, and it is an obstacle that can get in your way and even run into your face, etc. So it is interesting training for the defensive side.

5. **Composite Boxing** - This is a form of dueling in chin na. The freestyle element is used in order to see if one will not force things, but react with the knowledge learned in the form.

The Crown Eagle has been practiced by a few of our instructors for many years. Buddy Benford has done a lot of work with it and uses the form as a series of techniques to teach his principles.

Now the interesting thing is that Mr. Casey only taught me six sections, or about 60 movements. The material is so rich and full of techniques that the thought of knowing or practicing a 360 movement form seems crazy. We have had our fill for a long time with what was given to us.

As I say many times, chin na must fit into the Chinese Boxing encounter naturally so that it speeds up or enhances the road to the finish. It uses efficiency without the forcing of chin na when other things would be better. We include the Crown Eagle study at the end of our Chin na Board.

CHAPTER 26
TAI CHI CHUAN

DURING THE YEARS WITH CASEY, he spoke of Tai Chi often but didn't teach me any until about 1982. He said it was the Tao Ping Siang form at first; but after a little while, he said it was his martial version of the form. He referred to it as the Yang/Chen Synthesis. This is what Wang Shu Shen called his Tai Chi, but it was not the same form as Casey's.

Master Tao's form comes from Cheung Man Cheng, and as the years passed while learning from Master Tao, we also realized that he brought in some influence from the internal style he called Water Boxing.

When Casey first starting teaching me Tai Chi, he was watching me work on the first section and said, "There are so many things wrong with your Tai Chi that I don't know where to begin." That builds confidence! He did not teach it at a pace that was easy to follow, so I was struggling. Not long after, he told me he didn't have the patience to teach Tai Chi. It was difficult for Mr. Casey to learn Tai Chi, and it also proved to be one of the hardest things for me to learn. I usually learned at a pretty fast pace, and the detail and slowness of Tai Chi gave me a lot of trouble early on.

Mr. Casey gave me the film of Master Tao and said that I should memorize it first, and then he would teach me. That is what we did. Mr. Casey talked about Push Hands but did not teach me much about it. He showed the principle that he learned from Tao, but after he would yield, he would always come in and finish as if he was teaching Chinese Boxing all of a sudden.

Casey said that his martial form coming from the Tao form was influenced by Chen Style. He only knew Chen Style from a friend in Taiwan who studied from Tao but had learned some sort of Chen Style. This guy's Chen Style looked martial, but it did not seem to contain the main ingredients that I learned later from the Chen Family. At any rate, Casey taught that he included something in Tao's Tai Chi that he called recurve. Recurve was a type of spring-loaded, forward potential pressure. So if you were standing neutral and vertical and someone pushed you, the momentum would most likely knock you backward. When you "caught up with the results of the push, you would begin to go forward." If your body was in recurve, which would have just a hint of a forward lean, you would react differently. When pushed backward the same way, you would go back, but you recovered sooner and had an explosive spring movement forward. This is called recurve. This principle is actually used in practically all of our Chinese Boxing training.

Casey also made some changes to footwork in Tao's Tai Chi and practiced it fast and with martial rhythm and energy. So it definitely fit what Casey was teaching, but it was not the Tai Chi I would learn from Tao or from Chen Family.

I actually saw Casey practicing Tai Chi slowly a couple of times, and he actually looked pretty good. Master Tao really loved Mr. Casey, and that is probably the only reason he was so kind to me. One of my students asked Tao once what Mr. Casey's Tai Chi was like. Master Tao's answer was full of diplomacy when he said, "Mr. Casey died very young." I do think Tai Chi was difficult for Mr. Casey, but I also think he understood it and drew some things from it in his total synthesis martial art. Mr. Casey was not normally known for a lot of yielding, but he spoke of yielding as an important part of his art.

Master Tao Ping Siang

CHAPTER 27
MASTER TAO PING SIANG

MASTER TAO WAS one of Casey's main teachers. When Casey was studying the most, he would be with Tao all morning, and then in the evening he would be with Lo Man Kam. He spent time with the other masters in between, but they were the two with whom he spent most of his time.

After studying with Casey and the other Tai Chi teachers I have had, Casey was the most unlike the others. The reason I say that is because most of the application he showed me, regardless of the style, had much more projection and less passive yielding. But Mr. Casey could show and teach the Tao method. He attempted to get everything important that Master Tao treasured.

Cravens first meeting with Tao

Workshop in Tennessee with Master Tao Ping Siang

As noted previously, Casey passed in 1986, and two years later I moved to Florida. About the second year in Florida, I received a notice from a friend in New York that Master Tao was spending six months in Taiwan every year and six months in the US. Although Casey had met Master Tao in Seattle, he had studied with him in Taiwan. So there was a group in Seattle that brought Tao over. After a while, Tao would spend three months in Seattle as a base and three months in New York (at William Chen's school). William Chen and Master Tao were classmates under Cheung Man Ching and had lived with him for a few years. Tao was older than William and very humble and laid back with his philosophy, while William Chen had a desire to let people know that Tai Chi could be a serious fighting art.

Master Tao had a keen interest in fighting; but in his teaching through the years, he focused on the area of Push Hands. This practice involves receiving the force from your partner and making space with your movement and body so that the person pushing can continue pushing forward without interference. If the person pushing has any momentum, Tao was so soft that there was never a resistance to the push. So if the overextension and energy was given, then Master Tao would have numerous ways to follow up and throw a person down or out.

Master Tao teaching Push Hands

While staying in New York for three months each year, Tao was often hosted by Nathan Managed. Nathan was one of William Chen's top people and subbed for him sometimes when the seminar schedule got too busy. Nathan walked into my school in South Florida in 1989-90 when he was visiting his dad. We had an interesting meeting, and he showed interest in Chinese Boxing. He was also interested in pushing hands with me. Over time we became great friends. He often accompanied Master Tao on his seminars to Florida and Tennessee.

My connection to Tao for all those years of seminars was due to the fact that I was a student of Mr. Casey. I met Tao at a seminar in Indiana. We were upstairs in the dead of summer with no air conditioning, and he was teaching push hands. Everyone was sweating a lot, and he just laughed at us. It was a great experience; and due to some help from Nathan after the seminar, Tao agreed to come and teach our group. He came to Tennessee three or four times and to Florida about ten times. He also did a seminar for one of my students in Sacramental, California, which I attended. Afterward, I went back with Tao to Seattle and to the group that sponsored him to the US. It was good to spend time with some of the main people there.

I remember that things had a way of starting out badly with the teachers I eventually had. In Tao's case, all was good except for the time I wanted to take him to the best Chinese Restaurant in Fort Lauderdale on his first trip to Florida. Master Tao was so soft spoken that you had to stand pretty close to him to hear what he was saying. He knew a pretty good amount of English, but the softness of his voice often made it difficult for the student to catch everything he was saying. It was best when Nathan was there because he knew very well what Master Tao was all about. Anyway, we took him to the restaurant, and he ordered noodles. When the dish was brought to him, he seemed to get upset because it was not cooked the way he asked. Eventually, the cook came out and Master Tao had a very animated conversation with him. This was another side of Tao I was unaware of that he rarely revealed. He had a lot of fire in him, but it was easy not to notice because of his manner.

Later on, when I made the decision to study with Gaofei Yan in Chen Tai Chi, I didn't want Tao to find out through the grapevine. So when he was coming to one of my student's houses in Nashville for a seminar, I planned to tell him. When I first saw him, he came right up to me and said that he heard I was studying Chen Tai Chi. I answered yes. He asked who this person was that was teaching me. I mentioned his name, and then he asked me if he was soft. I answered that he was not as soft as you. Then we actually had a wonderful discussion about some things in Tai Chi. It turns out that he did some of the same things as Chen Tai Chi but had a different terminology for some of the same topics. I asked him about silk reeling, and he told me that his Tai chi always turned like a screwdriver.

In the end, he was like a father, worried that I was going down a very bad path. Interestingly, he taught me better in every way from that day on. He tried to explain more, and he corrected me more.

Right after the conversation that we had that day, Joe Rea Phillips was going to take his new German Shepherd for a walk. This was a highly bred Shepherd that was just a few months old. Two things happened that were very interesting. While walking in the park, Joe Rea looked as if he was holding on for life to keep the shepherd from running away. Master Tao, who probably wasn't a hundred pounds, went over to him to grab the leash. Joe Rea looked horrified, and all I could visualize was the dog taking off with Master Tao hanging on to the leash and flying horizontal through the air. But strangely, the dog calmed down a bit, and Master Tao was able to walk him fine.

There was a time the next day or so at Joe Rea's house, that he was in one room and lost the grip on his dog; and he took off running to the living room where Master Tao was sitting in a recliner. I thought the dog was going to jump right on top of him, but he had his feet up in the shape of a V and was able to get the dog's head between his feet. The dog fought to move around the feet, but Master Tao just followed his energy, and he finally got tired of trying about the time Joe Rea arrived. Tao was fearless, and I don't know if he knew the danger he was in.

Another experience with Master Tao involved a teacher who came to the seminar at Vanderbilt who was very nice, but we did not know him well. Once, while everyone was paired off practicing, one person went to the restroom, and the instructor who was left without a partner quickly stepped up and held out his hand to push with Master Tao. I was watching closely because I had no idea what this guy might have in mind. Sure enough, the instructor exploded a push on Master Tao that would have knocked him back a few feet if it had landed. Master Tao perfectly yielded and took the overextended push downward, and the guy landed on his knees, hitting the floor. The guy looked up and smiled and saluted him.

Now when lunch came and we were with Tao driving to a place to eat, he was very irritated that the guy had done what he did and considered it disrespectful. Then he told me to make sure to push with the instructor when we returned. I didn't know if he was commissioning me to be a hit man or what. Anyway, in the afternoon we finally got to pair up. I was on top alert for his explosion, but he never attacked; and when I pushed, he yielded way back, as he was a tall person in a pretty long stance. He seemed vulnerable for a sweep, but I didn't want to attack when he was yielding so much and staying away. That is the way he stayed and would not attack to give me a chance. Tao was ok with it later as he was watching what was happening.

Nathan and I enjoyed pushing hands with each other. It was a chance to test someone who had a lot of experience pushing with a lot of people from around the world that visited the William Chen studio in New York. Nathan was shorter than me, but stocky and tough and had a good root. So we would enjoy some back and forth friendly competition. In a couple of the early seminars when we got a little rowdy, Tao would walk over to us and look very serious and not happy. After a couple of times, we realized that it was not our place to play while he was trying to teach the entire class to yield. So we behaved from then on.

Now once I asked Tao about entering a push hands tournament in Washington. He told me that he didn't think it would be profitable. About the same time, we had another meeting at Vanderbilt, which was one of the last seminars with Master Tao. I was pushing with Nathan politely and not making a disturbance, which we had done for years. All of a sudden, Nathan exploded on me and knocked me back. I looked around and asked him what he was doing. He told me that Tao had told him that he should push strong with me because he didn't get the opportunity to push with people who could push very often. So we played that day, and Master Tao didn't care.

He had also told Nathan never to enter a push hands tournament. They were used to traveling together to a meeting in Taiwan that was a big gathering for Tai Chi workouts that held a tournament in remembrance and honor of Cheung Man Ching. On the flight to Taiwan, Master Tao asked Nathan if he had entered the tournament, and Nathan looked at him and told him he had never allowed him to. So Master Tao could definitely change his mind about things. He was most interesting.

One other time he was watching me push with someone at a seminar, and I was having some trouble figuring out which way to move. This was shortly after I had begun studying Chen Tai Chi. In general, you turn powerfully when pushed in Chen Tai Chi, and Master Tao wants you to make space for every push. He came over to me and told me that my problem was that I couldn't decide what movement to do. He was right; I was trying to figure it out at that time.

My conclusion over time is that the Chen method is a little more secure, and under pressure, I would tend to choose that method of dissolving the force. At the same time, I think it is very valuable to practice the Tao method. One of the instincts that we try and teach in Chinese Boxing is that our body should always be moving and reacting in a way that is evading force rather than staying still and dissolving things with the arms.

There are many stories I could recite about Master Tao. He was beloved and is missed by many of his students.

CHAPTER 28
FUKIEN WHITE CRANE

FUKIEN WHITE CRANE (Bai Ho Chuan) was taught to me by Mr. Casey. He taught the Hsieh style to me directly with three empty forms. It also included a Mook Form. The Chen Bai Ho Chuan was taught more like the Tai Chi was taught to me. He had me memorize from film that he had, and then made corrections to what I came back to him practicing. So my preference was the forms he taught to me directly. The difference in the two methods was that the Hsieh style emphasized strong structure and posture. The Chen Crane focused on mobility and footwork. They both had some common ground as well.

But the forms were not nearly the most important part of White Crane. White Crane taught a dynamic whipping projection. Some say it is like Tai Chi in that regard. Many of the exercises in White Crane used to develop this whip or tremor are pretty unusual. This shaking power was also used in their iron body development. The whipping of the forearm, hands and fingers is the central method of practice. They apply this energy to a big Wing arm movement which can have enormous power. They also use this shaking as a method of iron body development.

The White Crane methods seen in Taiwan are numerous. One characteristic seems to be that they all have little segments of forms and sets, but it is hard to find a school that seems to have the whole package. Admittedly, Mr. Casey's research was limited on time, but he did get a chance to train with the masters of these two styles, and they were quite good. In the Chinese Boxing boards, Mr. Casey drew a lot from Wing Chun and White Crane. In White crane it was the whip hand and the Wing Arm, along with some defenders.

Master Chen in Fukien White Crane

Probably Casey's favorite part of White Crane was the the Fukien Mook Form. In China this Mook had a post and two wooden arms that were held wide from the post like a double whip hand posture. He saw some Fukien schools that had a half post and two inner tube tires twisted and hooked to the bottom of the half post, stabilized on the ground and ceiling. That made the wooden post and arms very much alive and actually very dangerous to use. So fortunately, we had some people in our extended CBII Group that had the skills and materials to build Casey's idea of a Fukien Mook.

This Mook was more stable than the half Mook, but it was very powerful because of the springs that allowed the mook to pivot left and right. The more pressure applied on the mook, the more potential release was present. The arms could also move up and down from the end. The Mook form has a wonderful array of techniques that moves 360 degrees around the apparatus.

Fukien White Crane Mook Jong

The story that Casey gave about meeting the White Crane Chen Master was interesting. He took a translator to the first meeting. The meeting was arranged through the KFROC Republic of China. Casey had learned through the years that if a potential teacher asked you to demonstrate what you knew, you didn't want to look competent. Some teachers were skeptical of your intentions, and they didn't appreciate spies from other groups. So Casey did an Okinawan kempo form poorly. While he was performing, the two daughters of the master were giggling. When he was done, Master Chen told him through the translator that he was terrible and no good at martial arts. Casey simply told him that he knew that, and that was the reason he wanted to study with him.

The master proceeded to go to Mr. Casey and wrap him in a chin na lock and throw him to the ground. He then picked him up, only to throw him down again and again. After a period of time, it appeared that he was finished. He then spoke through the translator and told him he would teach him and where to meet him for his first class. Mr. Casey immediately asked the translator to find out what he should pay him for his services. The master responded that he thought he had just paid enough, referring to the session he had just endured. This teacher never charged Mr. Casey for the lessons he took from him.

Admittedly, he did not go to him as much as he went to Tao and Lo, but this was still quite unusual. A wealthy American in Taiwan at the time studying with various martial art teachers were often charged far more than what was charged to the people locally. I'm not saying this is not fair, but this teacher was unusual in this regard.

The old Taiwan 8 mm films revealed that Mr. Casey did have a film of this teacher and his daughters doing their art. He mentioned that he and his daughters went around Taiwan doing demos together. He was nicknamed by some as one of the five Tigers of Taiwan. In the films, his daughters performed the first six forms in his system. They are relatively very short forms. He performed the seventh. It was easy to see that he had a lot of skill. His daughters also performed a number of weapon forms that they practiced—Single Saber, Double-edged straight sword and two person sets involving the sabres and the spear. There was also a short clip of some empty hand drills that he was doing with his daughter.

There is a small list of people in CBII that have seriously studied this art. Some are still active with us, but I presently have only one student that comes to me regularly to study this art. I may not be the best person to teach these separate arts to those with a singular interest. I encourage the students to learn an internal art such as Tai Chi because of its great contributions, and I also require a certain amount of the Chinese Boxing basics in order to take the traditional forms and integrate them more quickly into the martial application. Application is not taught so much like the old one or two-step self-defense, but by putting the technique into a realistic flow with emphasis on entry, touch and finish.

CHAPTER 29
HAND/BODY TRAINING

WHEN MR. CASEY came to Chattanooga the first time in the early 70's, he taught a session in which we did iron body training. We did arm pounding and leg pounding. There were several normal weightlifting actions that involved holding the staff, and the helper had to hold the staff, creating resistance, so one would have to push or pull against the resistance.

That was before we started learning Chinese Boxing. When I was training in Connecticut, he taught me two kinds of hand training. The first was called *Interdiction Palm*. This was the training that Shaolin schools would typically do.—using the stamping, cutting, slapping, cutting and dotting hand strikes to hit apparatus such as sand bags, etc. Everything Casey did in training related back to the theory of his art and the principles.

Casey's interdiction palm had a couple of things that made it unique. The apparatus was a bag that used a softer burlap canvas and was full of ball bearings or BBs that were perfectly round. A large bag was the most desirable. In Chinese Boxing, the goal was to develop tough hands for combat without losing the sensitivity in the hands needed for touch. When one hit the bag, the bearings acted on each other and gave way, allowing a better response than hitting something that would not move. It allowed the force of the hit to absorb into the target and not bounce back into the one that was hitting.

The second thing was that all the strikes were done with a pattern. There was a point of contact and depth after the hit, and then some circular return pattern which promoted the idea of the apparatus absorbing rather than bouncing back energy. This is done on most all of our power strikes in Chinese Boxing.

In executing the pattern, it was important not to create a "rub" on contact, which would tend to cause blisters.

Interdiction Palm is a physical striking exercise (Yang), so one uses a Yin style jow or liniment to protect the hand from bruising, etc. A Yin jow was one that was formulated and then allowed to sit for a long time. It is often said that the longer it would sit, the better and more potent it would be.

The other kind of training was a Yin or more passive training. It was called _Yang Dar_ and required the use of a Yang jow. A yang jow was one that was cooked. It was strongest during the first 30 days, after which it would start weakening rapidly. The training involved having your hands sandwiched between two bags full of ball bearings or BBs that surrounded your hands. A board was put on top of the bags, and the weights were stacked on top of the board to increase the weight, putting pressure to squeeze your hands. There were a lot of precautions in setting up this training. So you would sort of hold a Peng body state, and then project out your fingertips while the weights squeezed. This was done five minutes daily. Then, one would thrust 30 times into a bucket of sand, using latex gloves. Intensity was achieved by adding weight.

Mr. Casey believed that this method enabled him to hit harder and penetrate more over time than the Interdiction Palm did. It is one of those things you would have to experience to get an idea. So it definitely would fall into the area of mind training.

The value of Hand/Body training can vary. If one is interested in just the health benefits of the art, it would not be necessary. If one wanted to compete in sparring or MMA, then there would be some training for the hands and body that could be beneficial. If someone needed to be fist fighting every day or so, then very heavy hand training would be necessary to avoid injuries.

All the hand or body training in the world will not help you dodge a punch or teach you to move into proper positions in fighting. In fact, hand training is one of the frostings. In general, if you want to be a fighter, you want your body to endure some striking and rough treatment, so iron body training could be helpful. Some people may fight with the majority of their technique being grappling, so they may not use their hands for striking. But it will be important to have some hand training if you are a fighter because there will be times when you will need to strike.

Hand training will not be your priority early in your training. It is much more important to develop your movement and posture and many basics in the martial study you have chosen.

CHAPTER 30
CASEY 1948 -1986

SO MY TIME with Mr. Casey was from 1972 until his death in 1986. Mr. Casey had a suspected brain tumor. I say suspected because he would not put most medicines in his body since he often reacted dramatically to medications. When he started having problems, he was unwilling to put the dye in his body to test what was happening. He died within about 3-4 months. He did not tell anyone besides his wife. In retrospect, there were small indications when I talked to him at night; but I was not in a position to ask his wife about it, so I didn't know.

You can imagine the reality check when something like this happens. Many of my students were in shock. Some were even bitter, feeling like we were cheated.

Yes, he could have taught us a lot more, but I didn't feel like I could judge what he was going through. He was pretty private about what went on the last four or five months of his life.

Mr. Casey had a different worldview than my own. His did not have much hope in looking forward. While life is in many ways a mystery with some big questions, one can live with hope or without it based on one's worldview.

U - Christopher Casey with James Cravens Group (1981)

I CERTAINLY FELT I was very close to Mr. Casey. I don't know if anyone could be really close outside his wife; but as he put it, he could stand being around me a little longer than most people. I mentioned that in the beginning, my time with him was uncomfortable; and although I totally enjoyed what he had to teach, I was always ready to go home after a few days of training. It was not only intense physically, but the mental pressure, especially at first, was difficult. He could be very condescending. Over time, he changed, and I saw a more natural side of him when he was more relaxed and around his wife. During that time, he was actually a lot nicer to be around and enjoyable.

With all the dedication he gave to learning and training, he did not teach many people. He taught some large military classes for a little while. He had the Georgia Tech club for a few years. He had a couple of key students in Atlanta that I spent time with, but they did not keep training with him after he left Atlanta. His father-in-law told me that he would start a class, and it would be large; but within a few classes, it had dwindled down to only a few. He felt himself an outcast to most of humanity. Maybe some of that was arrogance, but he was quite different and a very creative independent thinker. He had little tolerance for anyone's lack of discipline.

He taught Manfred Steiner for about a year and had a close connection to him since he taught him a lot in that one year. After that, they had a bit of a falling out for many years. Only at the end did they meet, shortly before his death.

T - Author with Chinese Boxing Association, Taiwan: (L to R) Chiao, C.H>, Lo Man Kam, Student, Ho Tse Hao, Author, Wang Shu-chin

KFROC in Taiwan welcoming Casey back in 1971

My sessions with him were about every three months. It was sometimes in hotels, etc., in the early years when he was moving around a lot. The best times for me were the years that he was in Stanford, Connecticut. I had a circuit of seminars that I was able to teach that took me to the Northeast, teaching in Pennsylvania, Connecticut and Long Island. Then I would spend a few days with Mr. Casey. He had a pretty elite job, advising his bosses on the political climate of the world and whether to take on various insurance and reinsurance contracts from all kinds of situations. At the time, his wife told me that insurance was pulling in about one dollar and paying out six. She said that Chris's company was pulling in six dollars and paying out one due to his advice and decision recommendations. She said there were just a few people in the world that did what he did and that he had become well known in this capacity.

When he resigned, he was very secretive about where he was staying for quite a while because he was being pursued by his company, hoping to get him to return.

So I felt very fortunate to have those years with him. Even though the training was every three months, Chris called me late at night for many years. It was not so much his choice, but it was the only time it would not interfere with my job or family. He mostly talked about martial arts, but we discussed other subjects as well. When teaching, he showed things on me, and that helped a lot. But the answers to my questions and clear understanding usually came later during our conversations. Without them, I would not have had a grasp on what was involved in his art, and the uniqueness it contained.

He passed at the age of 39, a few months shy of his 40th birthday. In some ways, he was like 80 in roads traveled and mind miles. He taught me a lot about critical thinking, which has nearly disappeared in our academic institutions. It was quite amazing what he discovered in his studies of the martial arts. His mind was able to take an average physical ability and help him develop incredible martial skills.

It has now been around 37 years since his passing. It's amazing how one could accomplish so much in such a short lifetime. Like all of us, he had strengths and weaknesses. Often, people that are mentally gifted like Mr. Casey would find trouble actually being productive in their lives. He was very productive in anything he decided to pursue. He was able to reach very high levels in martial art and his field of employment.

We often hear cliches like, "Money can't buy happiness," etc. Mr. Casey had money, but it didn't seem important to him. His pursuits and accomplishments did have meaning to him, although they did not seem to bring him any contentment or happiness. While I have high admiration for Mr. Casey's martial art creativity and accomplishments, I realize that something was missing in his worldview outlook. When he talked in depth about outlooks, he was often very depressing in his philosophy of life and the future. More on that later.

Christopher G Casey in 1981

CHAPTER 31
THE AFTERMATH OF A SAD INTERRUPTION

WHAT NOW?

Mr. Casey was gone, and he left a ton of material with me; but I did not feel in any way that I could continue what he taught. Credit to my students that had not been deterred. They kept studying from me, and that gave me energy and encouragement.

Soon I realized that I needed to organize what I had learned, or it would just be a bunch of stuff. I knew Casey had great skill to control another person physically in combat. But how could I get better, and how could I possibly teach his technique to someone else successfully?

I would never have the projection that Mr. Casey possessed. His method certainly made my projection a lot better, but I had to realize that all of us are different and have various strengths and weaknesses. There are some things that cannot be ignored in martial arts, and all methods must address these items. However, the method of Casey's boxing was not just one thing, such as his projection, etc. He taught a very comprehensive and coherent logical method when facing a life and death realistic situation. He also taught a set of principles that would enhance practically every part of the physical techniques needed in the art. If I could make the theory understandable and could demonstrate the value of the combined principles, then maybe something could happen to continue his art.

So, for the next two years and beyond, I formulated a few things. There was nothing new that I created, but I formulated the layout and outline of the Chinese Boxing Encounter. This involved the breakdown of Entry, Touch and Finish. The details were developed, and the goal was now to let everything that we learned in technique and style find its place in the Encounter. At that point, we had a numerous list of Techniques, and we could work on making them stronger. We could do several of the arts duels such as Chi Sao, push hands and joint hands, but that was not the realistic fight. Until we understood where these things contributed and belonged within the Encounter, it was going to be an art that never really became clear to those who tried to work at it.

The Encounter used critical thinking to understand where everything would have its place. So I won't talk about the Encounter in detail in this writing, but it was the piece and glue that I didn't have. I would revisit in my mind how Casey controlled me in a situation. He often said that touch is how the art is transferred. He mentioned that one must "remember" the touch. I would get a student to help, and sometimes I was just at a loss. I remember that he wasted little time getting an advantage on me, and then I couldn't catch up with him. He was not gifted physically, so I couldn't figure out what he was doing. As I analyzed the forward pressure aspect and how his body came at me, I realized that the forward pressure was a big key. I could remember how I felt as he completely overcame me and captured me.

One of the keys at this time was that I had to connect the Principles that Casey taught to how they related to the fighting techniques. For example, one could be rooted and lose every fight simply because he was not fast enough—or many other reasons. There are numerous examples of this involving the principles. What was missing from the principles was the understanding of how the Encounter worked.

Casey would constantly get a jump and advantage on me. Then I would feel this unbeatable force turn me, then capture; and once he captured, his projection would click in. Now I didn't have that kind of projection, so could I still do this? First, I wasn't even able to do the first part. So I began to study the concept of critical distance. I knew that if I could learn and get into critical position using deception and then use non-telegraphic explosion to attack, I would get the head start that Casey seemed to always get. Now I just said a mouth full because the study of how to close the gap is deep. But you don't have to always close it by offense. They can come to you as you do a Yield and Counter action or a Stop Hit. If you learned to do the timing well, you would get a head start in all of these strategies. So the study of Entry started to be broken down into something of a science.

When I got the advantage, I would frequently lose it. So then I realized that the principles of root and body state were necessary. By using excellent footwork, one could apply forward pressure when moving from the rooted advantage; and if one developed some touch skills, one could capitalize on the forward pressure to turn someone or create an opening. So the principles all worked to enhance each other and make for the magic that occurs when that happens. Good idea—but it would take a lot of experimentation. There had to be cooperation at first, and that had to develop into a freestyle environment where the reality of this could be tested.

That was what was happening in 1987 and for the next few years.

I am grateful that everything didn't stop with the death of the founder. The truth of the message was superior to the people that studied it.

Another thing missing in our culture is the confidence that truth exists. We always referred to our boxing as "truth in combat." It was supposed to be a motto that meant that we would not necessarily be tied to tradition or what our teacher said, but we would continue to seek and examine for what was true or real in combat.

PART THREE
FLORIDA 1988 - 2012 CHINA

CHAPTER 32
FLORIDA 1988

Jack Lannom on right.

SO IN 1988 I got an offer from Jack Lannom to come down and teach at his school. He would handle the business and selling, and I would do the teaching. The offer was good even though it didn't last. It started on a high note, and I moved the family down toward the end of the year. I met a lot of great people, and outwardly the school was thriving. I taught about 100 students privately twice a month and also taught some of the group classes. Mr. Lannom was having some difficulties, and after a year we agreed that we should go different directions in order for things to work out. Several students who became longtime students helped me get out of the situation. It took a couple years of trying different methods, but finally things started to normalize.

In the second year, I was teaching what we called the Long Boards. It included almost every curriculum Casey had taught me, and there were dozens of items on all sixteen boards or categories. This was a pretty large overstep. In the effort to preserve everything, I had produced a curriculum that was unachievable for most people. This would not work. So after a year of teaching this curriculum, I chiseled down the material to a curriculum that was more realistic at mastering. I settled into a curriculum we called the Chinese Boxing Core Synthesis, which had 16 Boards with about 12 items on each one.

Although the Long Boards were something of a blunder, it turned out to be an important stage of learning for me personally. I had come to understand at the time that just because you know more techniques and forms does not mean that your art is very good. Recognizing the mistake and then going through the mental process of choosing the core items that were necessary was one of the greatest educations that I experienced. It helped put me in a position to begin making real progress in the aftermath of the passing of Mr. Casey. He was not going to be there to answer my questions directly, so I had to use the critical thinking I was taught and depend on recalling and remembering all the physical things, especially all the conversations in which he gave me the bird's-eye perspective on what I was learning.

For students who had some background in martial arts, the new Short Core Synthesis curriculum was mostly achievable in a couple of years. The ability to learn the Chinese Boxing Encounter well with applications along with the principles was the part that would take a little longer. We had a small core of people that started developing the Chinese Boxing of Casey that was based on the study of the Encounter and the Principles. It was a growing time for me, and it was a time in which I was able to consolidate what the boxing was that I had learned from Mr. Casey. I am thankful for how he demonstrated it on me, and I am thankful for the years where the puzzle was put together to a practical art.

Casey would ask me at times how many students I had that were *suns* and how many were *moons*. Suns were sources of creative thought, and moons were those who simply reflected the teacher. Neither one is necessarily a negative thing, but one should attempt to be creative so that the knowledge and art is is personally owned by the student and not just recorded.

Another way that Casey explained it was as a philosopher. He said that "one should think the thought that the thinker thought when he thought the thought." Philosophy can be summed up with a huge question mark because it always asks the question ***why***. Why did the person or group that put this in their art find it necessary? Does this fit into the overview of the art, or does it come into conflict? It is tapping into the creative juices that you were given. We are all different, and some function more comfortably as moons, but there is a certain amount of independent thought and ownership that each student should obtain.

On the other hand, some people think they are a mighty sun and are God's gift to martial arts; they feel every idea they have is genius. That is why one should be humble and seek to look at things as objectively as possible. The art must be coherent in theory and achievable by the average person. This requires some honesty, which at times is very difficult. I have been teaching before when the student actually comes up with something that refutes what I am teaching. By instinct, I want to defend my position, but sometimes simply staying open and reflecting on what is said will bring one to a different conclusion.

The Florida move was, in the long picture, something that was good for my family and me. It certainly didn't seem so for quite a while. I have to say that God was gracious with me as I made mistakes and was very forgiving, allowing me to make adjustments. I had to work so much for many years that I probably did not give my family the attention and time I should have. My wife was excellent in filling in that gap; but if I had made better decisions from time to time, I would have been able to prevent this lack of balance.

CHAPTER 33
THE FORMING OF THE TEN PRINCIPLES

ONCE THE OUTLINE of the Encounter was developed, I was stimulated by the one who brought me down to Florida to organize the principles of Chinese Boxing. I had never counted them but just referred to them.

Jack Lannom, who hired me to teach in his school back in 1988, was a salesman and marketing guy. He asked me all these questions about Chinese Boxing. He asked me how many principles there were in Chinese Boxing, and I told him I didn't know; I would have to think about it. I came back to him and told him that there were nine Principles. His response was that there needed to be ten principles for marketing purposes. At any rate, I went back through everything and came up with ten—Rooting, Yielding, Body State, Unitary movement, 6/9 Changeability, Line and Angle, Forward Pressure, Centeredness, Projection and Mind Hit.

As time went on, I was never satisfied with the number. I would think and think about how to change it, and possibly to reduce it. There is some overlapping; but the harder I tried to improve it, I just ended up deciding to keep it as it was.

Some things did change and evolve. As I was introduced to Silk Reeling, I began to learn that it was a pretty big deal. So I thought about adding number eleven to the list. As I thought about it, I realized that silk reeling is a connected and unified movement, so it fit perfectly with the unitary theory.

The principle of Centeredness has a number of meanings, and I thought about including it under the 6/9 theory. Though it seems to fit, I never pulled the trigger on that one. Forward Pressure is definitely a principle in the encounter, but I had thoughts about dropping that one from the list. Actually, line and angle, forward pressure and centeredness I thought would combine well into one principle that I would call *efficiency*. I never pulled the trigger on that one either. Maybe I will make some changes in the future. It is just that principles are not worlds on their own. They must work together to produce the special synthesized product. It is important to understand the principles in terms of how they work together to enhance the technique, movement and strategy that we use.

Casey never numbered the principles. And in breaking all of the martial art knowledge down, you could list over a 100 principles that one follows in a particular art. The thing Casey always encouraged me to do was to reduce and simplify concepts and principles into their smallest common denominator. He called this parsimony, and it is sometimes called Occam's Razor. It is the principle of desiring simplicity and clarity.

CHAPTER 34
GAOFEI YAN AND CHEN QUANZHONG

BEFORE CASEY DIED, he had spoken to me about Chen Tai Chi. He had a friend in Master Tao's class in China who did Chen Style, and Casey was impressed with its martial nature. He even included the martial aspect into his Kai Sai Tai Chi, which was his version of Master Tao's form. Casey added some footwork, a martial rhythm and a forward lean that was almost unnoticeable.

> **He called the lean recurve, which was a spring-loaded energy ready to prevent one from being knocked backward so easily without a returning energy or spring.**

Anyway, before he died, he told me that if I ever found someone who could teach me Chen Tai Chi, I should do it.

Fast forward to 1994-1995. A man named Gaofei Yan walked into my school to introduce himself and see what was going on in my school. He was very nice, and we ended up having a long conversation. He asked if I would demonstrate the Tai Chi I taught. So I demonstrated Master Tao's method of Tai Chi. He then demonstrated his Chen Family Style Tai Chi.

I had seen some Chen Style more frequently on the internet.

There was one teacher in particular who had some videos for sale. He actually had videos on all the internal arts. Anyway, he was very strong and flexible. In my mind, if I never found a Chen Tai Chi teacher, then maybe I could study this man's Tai Chi from his videos and see if I could get any insights from the movement. The one thing that I didn't like about this man's Tai Chi was that there seemed to be something lacking in his Fajing and demonstration of power. It was wiggly, and not in the best way. So I was refraining from trying to learn it when Gaofei Yan walked in.

Gaofei Yan - My first Chen Tai Chi teacher.

When he was moving through the form, there was nothing fancy; everything was very solid and quite powerful, especially for someone who probably weighed about 125 pounds. His fajing was solid and not phony looking. So I was impressed, and after he left, I began thinking about asking him if he would teach me Chen Tai Chi. After a few days, I decided to write him a letter. In the letter, I asked him some questions. I asked him if his Tai Chi was for health or for martial. Since I was so wedded to the martial, I wanted to know his thoughts on this. I asked several other questions as well.

He ended up popping into my school again. I was surprised. He had the letter in his hand and said that he wanted to answer the questions in person. I was very satisfied with his answers, so I asked him if I could study the art with him. He agreed, and I began private classes twice a week.

As I began to learn the Chen Style, I began to find some things that Mr. Casey and Master Tao had not emphasized. One of the more significant differences concerned keeping the lower back straight in Tai Chi. Both Chen and Yang styles believed in a straight lower spine, but they had different ideas about achieving it. In the Yang style, as well as the other arts that I learned from Casey, they believed in a tucked hip so that the hip caused the lower spine to angle forward. Some of Casey's teachers taught this, but did not show a tucked hip most of the time in their movement and postures. Others, such as Lo Man Kam, had a very exaggerated forward angled tucked hip.

Gaofei Yan and Uncle Chen (Chen Quanzhong)

At any rate, in Chen Style and many of the internal arts, the lower spine is achieved by sinking the tailbone. During the sink, the tailbone does not tuck forward but pivots slightly, maintaining a straight body. A curve in your lower back is a natural thing, but muscles often develop that begin to exaggerate the curve, and muscles are developed to support this extra curve. When one begins practicing straightening the spine with the Chen method, things relax; and the lower spine straightens, and the tailbone at the end will angle forward naturally.

This idea of straightening the back was spoken of in one classic which had been interpreted in recent times by tucking the hip. Doing this actually locks the hip. Instead of the crease going inward to open the hip, it locks up. So generally, when joints are locked, it takes longer to change position.

At first I believed the tucked hip as done in Wing Chun and Tao's Tai Chi was necessary for Chinese Boxing. As time went on, I had to admit that one would be more changeable and relaxed by doing it the way Gaofei was teaching. This wasn't just the Chen way; it was done in many internal arts. I honestly could not find an advantage in doing it the Yang way. Not everyone in Yang teaches it this way, but the connections that I happened to have were doing so.

Another major issue that was new to me was that of keeping the feet flat, focusing on the bubbling well as a point of balance. It was necessary that the Kua remain open when doing this. This helped prevent the inward cutting of the knee, which rested the rear foot in fighting closer to the edge of the foot rather than flat. I was concerned that if I did it the Yang way in fighting, I would lose my ability to explode forward while doing a shuffle A. I thought the cut knee was one of the reasons for the explosion that was so critical for good entry. As I studied this problem, I began to realize that by having the dan dian more to the front leg, it didn't matter if you had a foot on its edge or if it was flat. The takeoff was better in either position.

Another new development in my study was that I believed that the special concept of Silk Reeling could be integrated into our Unitary Theory. To have the whole body connected by *spiraling movement* was intriguing. I realized that sometimes in the various arts we practiced, we had silk reeling going on. For example, you rarely hear teaching coming from Pakua schools about silk reeling, but it is hard to deny that the movements of Pakua are perfectly set up for silk reeling.

Another thing I learned from this art was how the silk reeling was excellent for escaping an opponent's attempt to control you. One of my students had a private class with Chen Bing one year. My student was very good in chin na, so he wanted to show Chen Bing some of the locks and find out whether there were any escapes from these locks. In that hour my student got quite a few of the locks on his partner, and Chen Bing responded with a silk reeling escape. The person would have to be very good and experienced at the silk reeling actions that go through the whole body. If the student could respond instantly, then these were wonderful escapes. My student said that he only questioned if it could be developed good enough to happen in real time. I was amazed that I had learned a lot of escapes that were not nearly as efficient as the ones that Chen Bing taught.

I remember when another one of my students was in an Uncle Chen Quanzhong class back in the 1990's here in the states. My student was very excited with the chin na techniques that Uncle Chen was teaching. Uncle Chen noticed and mentioned to my student that it wasn't the particular technique that was so important, but that it was the ability to do silk reeling throughout the whole body at any time.

It was because of Gaofei that we met Chen Quanzhong, his teacher from China. Chen Quanzhong was certainly a special person. He could not speak much English; but when he was teaching, he was so clear in his movement and in his animated teaching technique that there was little doubt what he wanted you to do. When he visited us, it was his first time ever outside of China. That made a lot of his responses very interesting. When he was in South Florida, he asked us where all the people were. He was so used to masses of people where he lived in China that he wondered where they were hiding.

One time a student from another area came to one of Uncle Chen's seminars, and at one of the breaks, this student wanted to push on Uncle Chen. We made a partial attempt to protect Uncle Chen from the unknown student, but he would have no part of it. He wanted to allow the guy to push on him. The guy pushed very hard on Uncle Chen. Uncle Chen shifted to his rear leg and turned while receiving the two-handed push. Catching the student's arms, he rotated his waist and threw the guy, turning 270 degrees. He had kept feet and knees in the same position while doing this, and because the guy pushed hard, he also was thrown a pretty good distance.

Once at another student's house out of town, the student brought Uncle Chen into his garage, where he had some iron palm bags set up for striking on a table. He asked Uncle Chen if he hit apparatus. Uncle Chen said that he hit trees. He kept looking at the iron palm bags and went over and faced them. He began doing the large frame silk reeling pattern that he had been teaching in the seminars. He did it for a little while single hand. Then as he circled his arm, he led the pattern into a path to hit the bags without stopping. His energy was continuous, and he would come around and hit it over and over. His movement had an inward pattern and was not creating direct feedback into his body since it didn't bounce back from the contact.

In Washington DC when we were taking him around town, he wanted to see the White House, so we took him there for the tour. When we walked out of White House, he turned and asked Gaofei where Bill Clinton was. He proceeded to look at a vendor as we were leaving and seemed intrigued with some hats that were FBI and CIA hats that were for sale. We ended up getting him a CIA hat, and took some pictures of him wearing it. Ironically, it was same time a big news story was breaking in the US about a Chinese person who worked at one of the nuclear facilities and had been arrested for stealing a bunch of secrets from the United States.

There were also some stories about eating since Uncle Chen enjoyed some of the things that were new to him. At one location, the host offered him some chocolate cake. He had a piece, and then proceeded to eat the whole thing.

He was a very healthy person for his age. When he did the first seminar in South Florida in the early 90's, he started the warm-up by doing knee rotations in which you put your feet together with hands on the knees and begin rotating them together in a circular motion. He was bent forward so that his thighs were parallel to the ground. He circled and circled, and it seemed like he would never stop. Then he stopped and started going the other way for an eternity as well. All in one warm-up exercise, he proved who had the strongest legs in the room.

Also in that seminar after the warm-up, he wanted to see everyone do Laojia Yilu. Our group was in the process of learning the form. I think there were just two of us present who knew the whole thing. So as everyone came to their last movement, they would sit down. The funny thing was, when we started doing the form, Uncle Chen started talking to Gaofei loudly; and it sounded like he was not happy and also like he was scolding Gaofei. After a minute, he got quiet and continued to watch. There were just two of us left, and we were going up on one leg doing Golden Rooster. We heard Gaofei say, "Uncle Chen has seen enough." We always laughed about that. We were all standing there; Uncle Chen began to talk in Chinese, and then Gaofei started to translate. Gaofei cleared his throat and spoke very slow and pronounced. He said, "Uncle Chen wants you to know how happy he is that everyone is practicing Chen Tai Chi." Now that was really something, so we thought something was lost in the translation. I thought he was probably telling Gaofei that he did not understand how any group could be so bad at Tai Chi, and he was blaming Gaofei for it. We will never know for sure, but we always smile when we think about those days.

On his second trip, Uncle Chen taught me privately the second Form, Laojia Paocui (Cannon Fist). That was certainly a great privilege. We did it while traveling around to four cities and doing various seminars.

After that visit from Uncle Chen, Gaofei put together a book about Laojia Yilu. Gaofei took the pictures, and I put the book together on a computer; then we had about a hundred copies made. Gaofei also did some filming of Uncle Chen on that trip. Using the ACT organization (American Chen Tai Chi), he put together some of the filming we had done of Uncle Chen. He sold an empty hand tape of Uncle Chen doing Laojia Yilu and Laojia Erlu. In addition, he put together a second tape of Chen Tai Chi Weapons with Uncle Chin demonstrating most of them.

Another interesting tidbit was that when Uncle Chen demonstrated, he also showed another way to practice the form Laojia. It was what he called the "live form." It mostly followed the first section of Laojia, but he did it fast and very martial. It was beautiful to watch, and it made me think that he would have understood Casey's personal Tai Chi, which was also done fast and with martial energy.

Uncle Chen - Chen Quanzhong - 19dth Generation Chen

Although Gaofei taught me a lot of Chen Tai Chi, Uncle Chen certainly was wonderful. In demonstrating the large version of Tai Chi, he had a very unique Silk Reeling pattern compared to the main guys in Chen Village. Uncle Chen had several teachers, but they were from other places other than Chen Village, so that is why it looked so different. The silk reeling emphasized the vertical circle rather than the horizontal circle favored by several of the Chen Village teachers.

Gaofei did not promote himself when it came to Chen Tai Chi; he was happy to push his teacher to the front. The founding of the American Chen Tai Chi Association followed what Uncle Chen wanted to do in promoting the art in the U.S. Even though he took a back seat, Gaofei was a wonderful student of Tai Chi. He had one of the largest libraries of martial art when he was in China. It was fascinating for me to hear him discuss the theory behind the art of Tai Chi, as well as some of the philosophy. I feel fortunate because Gaofei had such a passion for Tai Chi, he would answer just about any question and talk about Tai Chi for long stretches. I think I would never have been so lucky getting the information from one of the older masters, or at least not as quickly.

James Cravens and Chen Quanzhong

CHAPTER 35
THE MISSING PIECES

CHINESE BOXING IS an awesome art that is unique, and I have always felt special to have learned it. Even so, after learning the internal style of Chen Taiji, I felt like there were areas of the Chinese Boxing that could be improved. Though not so much in the area of combat, there were definitely things the body could improve that would translate into more efficiency. The body structure of keeping the bones lined up provided for an alignment that would give the most when it came to projecting or even defensive positions.

Changes, such as a hip that sinks the tailbone with a lower spine pivot (rotating dan dian) and to keep the kua open constantly and be connected with the silk reeling movement, were all things that I thought would enhance the Chinese Boxing. I figured that it could be integrated if these things did not take away anything from the efficiency of Chinese Boxing. After all, the majority of the ten principles were taught in Chen Tai Chi. Not everything is the same in the two arts. There are some slight differences, such as separating when it comes to the finishing aspect of Chinese Boxing. Ending the fight with fajing was okay, but in Chinese Boxing we normally did a lot more to secure the finish.

I became convinced of these alignment improvements to the

body, so I spent a couple of years trying to make the adjustments more habitual. Of course, that means unlearning some things. I also took these things into my other arts, such as Pakua, Hsing-i, Walu, Wing Chun and White Crane. These postural rules are things that are universal truths concerning alignment and can only make the arts better.

CHAPTER 36
GERMANY AND CBII

Detlef Zimmermann - Hannover, Germany

IN 1999, a student of Manfred and Detlef in Germany came over for a vacation and tried to look me up in Florida. He wanted to work out with my group. His name was Stephen, and he was a student of Detlef.

It turns out that the German CBII guys who had been students of Manfred did not know much about the CBII group in the US. Stephan was a tall, lanky young martial artist. You could tell that he had a lot of emphasis on centerline training. His footwork was mostly shuffle A, as in Wing Chun.

Detlef Zimmermann and James Cravens

When he met with me, he asked to do push hands. At the time, his push hands was more to blast the centerline like he was doing Wing Chun Chi Sao. He was talented and had a very long reach. I think he got a different perspective of the Chinese Boxing practiced by the Group in the US.

Evidently, he persuaded Detlef Zimmermann to invite me over when he returned home. Starting in 1999, Rick Lupe and I took four trips, the last one in 2008. We made some good friends in Germany with Detlef and Wolfgang. Eric Metz was also there and, in recent years, has joined our CBIA group.

Detlef was a wonderful host and took us on sightseeing tours of castles, etc. He and his wonderful wife fed me a traditional German dinner that was outstanding. This was all in Hannover, Germany. This was the place that Casey had worked for a year before moving back to the states in 1981 and beginning the Chinese Boxing Institute International.

Detlef's School in Hannover Germany

On each of my trips, they arranged for me to have a nice meeting and meal with Manfred Steiner. On the last trip, Manfred invited me to his house for lunch, and his wife wrapped a couple of rattlesnakes around mine and Rick's necks. That was interesting.

Also on the last trip, Eric Metz and Dirk Wetter hosted us for a couple of seminars more north, in Hamburg, where they had a new school together. We met some nice people and had a great time there as well.

Eric Metz and Dirk Wetter Group in Hamburg, Germany

Manfred had primarily focused on Wing Chun/JKD concepts in his teaching of his former students. Once Casey died in 1986, Manfred basically quit teaching and left Detlef in charge of the school. He continued his own journey and ended up with a couple other students.

I'm not sure if I contributed anything to the Germany group, but I tried to develop the footwork and the concept of the Chinese Boxing Encounter. In the Tai Chi, I tried to develop the concept of Yielding and body movement. In the Pakua and Hsing-i, it was mostly mechanical data they learned.

Today, Detlef is following his own path but still promotes the CBII.

CHAPTER 37
CHEN XIAOWANG

AFTER BEING with Gaofei for several years, our pathways began separating a bit. It was not at all a bad separation. He was always helpful and kind to me.

Another person named CP Ong was someone who was promoting three of the four Buddha Warrior instructor/masters from Chen Village in their seminar tours in the U.S. He was a facilitator and would often travel with them in order to help with cooking and communication. One day, CP sent out an email to his mailing list, asking if anyone wanted to start having seminars with either Chen Zhenglei, Zhu Tiancai or Chen Xiaowang.

Since I was separating from Gaofei and the ACT organization, I was looking for someone to continue my Chen Tai Chi studies. CP especially wanted me to learn from Chen Zhenglei since he was CP's direct teacher. I had met Chen Zhenglei and Zhu Tiancai when we brought them in for seminars with the American Chen Taiji Association.

I had always been intrigued with Chen Xiaowang. I had seen him on video and loved the way he moved. I thought he was very athletic and moved in a pronounced martial energy when he did some of the faster motions of Chen Tai Chi. His fajing looked like top quality. I had always heard that he was pretty expensive to host for seminars, so I didn't think I had a chance to start bringing him over. But I emailed CP back and asked him. He said that Chen Xiaowang had only one spot available, so he didn't know if he would accept. CP called back within a few minutes, and we scheduled our first seminar with Chen Xiaowang in Tennessee. Before the seminar, he was teaching in Jacksonville, Florida, at Kam Lee's school, and I learned that he was available for private lessons. So I went to take a private class and participate in a chin na session group class that he was teaching at Kam Lee's school. I had written him a letter that CP delivered, explaining my background in martial arts. I thought he had read it when I drove up to Jacksonville, but he doesn't read English; CP said he read it to him. At any rate, my experience with him was interesting.

I had always, if given a chance, told the instructor what I wanted to learn. Casey had given me the opportunity to do that, so I was kind of spoiled. But as the years went on, I realized some of my folly and so began just asking Casey to teach me whatever he wanted. I was just interested in learning to do the things that made Casey so special. So when I met Chen Xiaowang that day, to my surprise, he asked me what I wanted to do. He also mentioned that from the letter, he saw that I had a martial interest in Tai Chi. I think that if asked, he probably would have worked with me on Push Hands or application. But from past experience, I told him I just wanted to do whatever the most important things that would help me accomplish his goals in Tai Chi. He asked me if I was used to doing Wuji. I had done some Wuji with Gaofei. Probably the maximum time I would practice Wuji was 20 minutes, so I said yes.

He told me to start standing in Wuji, and after a while, he would correct me. My ego led me to a problem. I had seen one of Chen

Xiaowang's videos in which he was standing in a low Wuji with the feet wider than normal. Wanting to impress him with my leg strength, I chose to start in a low Wuji. I felt my legs could take it. So he told me to close my eyes and practice. That was when a strange thing happened to me. I was standing there for a while, and then something started shaking in my lower body. I knew my legs were ok, but it was an uncontrollable shake in the hip/lower spine area that felt like my nervous system was out of sorts. Yes, the embarrassing type. This started at about the 20-minute mark, so I didn't know where he was; and even when I peeked, I didn't see him. So after shaking a while, he walks up to me and starts adjusting my hip and back area. Within a minute, he had stopped the shaking. That was interesting. He also decided to tell me to come closer in a shoulder width Wuji, which was more what I was used to and should have been doing from the beginning. Things were better, but he left me there for a total of forty-five minutes. Then he got in front of me and began doing Single hand silk reeling and told me to follow him.

Grandmaster Chen Xiaowang 19th Generation Chen Taiji

He was in front of me and looking in a mirror, so he could see how I was following. When Gaofei taught me, he mentioned one day that when you shift weight you should sink, and that would lead to a proper shift. At that time, I would shift several ways, and sinking to shift was just one of them. So I took it to heart and realized that if you elevate while shifting, there is more chance of losing your root; and if you did it in Push Hand, one could drive you away. If you sank before shifting, you would be in your legs very heavy; and with the turning of the body, you could neutralize some very powerful pushes. This was a big deal to me. So as I was silk reeling leg to leg, I made sure that I was sinking before every shift. He was watching me and, of course, to do the sink, I would have to come back up in order to sink again. Well, if you didn't do that you would drive yourself toward the ground. But he stopped me as I was coming upward and said no, stay down and level. I had seen him on tape and wondered why he didn't seem to sink and then shift.

So I stayed level, and my legs got very heavy. I had been coming up to take a breath, so to speak, before sinking down and shifting. Ok, so that was different from what I was used to with Gaofei. Uncle Chen had a very exaggerated up and down movement during silk reeling. That method would also be very hard work for the legs when doing about a hundred repetitions. But now, just staying down was a different kind of very difficult.

This changed my Tai Chi a lot. I asked Master Chen if he believed in sinking in order to shift. He said yes and that he did it, but it was a very small action. So this all gave me a new perspective and practice. I am appreciative of the way I was taught in the large frame from Gaofei and Uncle Chen, but all the large movement I had exaggerated, finding ways for my body to get rest. It was harder to relax with the large movement, and I had not calmed my body with all the extra twisting and up and down movement. So Chen Xiaowang taught what I really needed at the time—a calming movement. It was still difficult on the legs, but it allowed me to start relaxing my upper body. It was a perfect adjustment. Large movement and twisting I think is needed to open the body and feel its potential. Then you pull back so that the body is more relaxed, and the energy and chi will flow much better. Gaofei had told me that Uncle Chen's method was very good for opening up the body. The Chinese Boxing practice had closed me up some since there was less emphasis on opening up the stances, etc.

So after the silk reeling, the class was over, and he showed me some applications, knowing that my interest was in the martial. He asked me to push on him. I pushed with two hands at the chest. He kept asking me to push harder. His root was impressive. This part I was used to with Casey, but it was nice to get verification from another master that it was a necessary part of the art.

Walking out of the class he said, "You have a problem with your right foot." I disagreed, so he stopped and told me to get back into Wuji. I did and he pointed at my right foot and said "see." I looked down and thought my feet looked symmetrical. On closer inspection, I detected that my right foot was a couple of degrees toed out. I said ok and pulled in the foot, but I didn't see it as a very big deal. He then said, "Don't worry, most people over 50 go either right or left." So he told me to practice and keep the feet symmetrical.

When I went home, I spent the next few days looking down at my feet—and it was true. I had a pronounced right toe-out. I tried doing the Wuji with the feet parallel, and then the right foot started hurting pretty badly. So I was pretty close to not doing it anymore when it started to ease up and then went away.

So the first lesson didn't have a lot of action, but it was quite a lesson for me; it began my journey with Chen Xiaowang.

Chen Xiaowang working on his calligraphy.

Chen Xiaowang was a good teacher. I was told by some that all these teachers hold back and will not teach you the important things;

but as I got to know him more and more, I realized and appreciated that he had a quality that I was interested in. He had made a discovery earlier in his life that stayed with him, and it is probably the reason he has been respected for his high quality of movement and strength.

Someone else told me this story. Chen Xiaowang lost his parents to the government when he was just a kid—around 10 or so. That sort of left him as the head of his local family. So he dealt with all this for several years. After a number of horrible years in which the government mistreated certain families, things finally got better. His skills became recognized, and he won some competitions. Eventually, all this got him a better job offer with the government.

Chen Xiaowang with South Florida Group

Back in that time, normal people could not travel around China. This job allowed him to travel and be a consultant for the Wushu organization. As he traveled, he was able to visit many of the Chen Family members that were in other cities and teachers who had been scattered from the village for various reasons. As he met with various members of the Chen Family, he was always curious as to what he had missed or not been taught. He found that most of these people were seeking and would ask him the same question. So he was practicing and meditating on Tai Chi one day, and he had sort of an enlightening moment. He realized that all movement comes from the dan dian throughout the body and to the end of the body.

He rushed to talk to his cousin, Chen Zhenglei, and said he had discovered the secret or essence of Tai Chi. He told him that all movement starts at the dan dian and moves throughout the body. Chen Zhenglei sort of looked at him and him went "duh." Chen Xiaowang had been taught this, but it was different to know it in your head and then to have the knowledge transfer to your body.

All people who study with Chen Xiaowang know that he insists on perfecting the postures and strengthening the legs. Without both of these things, one can never feel what he wants you to feel. So if you look at all the top masters, many of them are very good. One thing that drew me to pursue Chen Xiaowang was his nearly flawless posture and strength, which seems to excel over most the others. Of course, this my opinion. With some of the others, there is an emphasis on learning a lot of things. Chen Xiaowang doesn't care what movements you're working on, he wants to remove the inconsistencies in your posture.

If you look at some of the earlier films of Chen Xiaowang, you will see a lot of strength and a much flashier performance in which his upper trunk moves out of vertical a lot more. As the years progressed, you see just a solid, more perfect vertical position. Because of the relaxation that is achieved from such a straight posture, he can move quickly with very impressive power and speed.

Another thing that attracted me to Chen Xiaowang was that in some of his demonstrations in which he went faster, I could see a very martial rhythm to his movement. Since I was from a martial background, that also was a reason I pursued him.

Now the Chen Family in recent years, or at least the younger generation, has worked hard toward developing the fighting aspect.

Was this aspect lost during the early days of the present government? Tai Chi was outlawed for about ten years. It's hard to know the answer since they practiced in secret. The focus at the time was more on survival, as hunger was a problem. At any rate, most of the application we have seen from the Chen masters has been one on one. The silk reeling responses are very effective to dissolve force, and then the application usually ended with a fajing.

So early on, one of the questions I had for Chen Xiaowang about real fighting concerned how fights are usually finished in Chen method. We had a little trouble communicating my question, but then his eyes got bigger and he said, "You mean war." So he told me that he had already told me the answer. If you are on balance, you could finish however you wanted. If you were off balance, you would not be able to finish at all. Of course, in Chinese Boxing we go to the finish, which is sometimes hitting but often is capturing and using destructive force during the capture.

My opinion is that when you do a classical fajing you have to be at a perfect distance in order to deliver the shock force. For most people, it would be low percentage to expect them to finish a fight with a fajing. So I was also encouraged when he told me that when he punches in real fighting, he tries to drive the fist completely through the opponent's body. I thought this was a different perspective than what we usually see from the Chen masters. It is a point of view that is closer to what we do in Chinese Boxing.

Of course, Chen Xiaowang's big influence on me was the importance of the basics. I was always the student that wanted to learn everything, and volume was important. Now I should have learned this lesson completely with Casey. He would ask me to do something I had learned, and then he would always go back to the first move and show me what I was missing. So he pointed me toward this direction, but Chen Xiaowang cemented it into my thinking—probably because Tai Chi is slow and grinding and takes a lot out of the body, so the basics have to be good. There are so many small and subtle corrections; and if you don't feel it, you will not remember it. As a teacher, it is sometimes hard to keep people's interest when you spend a lot of time on the basics. Of course, it is good for them, but you also don't want to lose your students because they get bored. So it is a challenge to teach Tai Chi.

The first year we had Chen for a weekend in Florida and then a week in Murfreesboro, Tennessee. We picked him up at the airport and took him to his hotel. Somehow while getting the luggage out of the car, the trunk got slammed on his fingers. I was already headed toward the hotel entrance, and a couple of other guys were helping with the luggage. I heard my students kind of gasp and ask Chen Xiaowang if he was alright. He was dripping blood from his finger. When I turned around, he was looking at his hand, then he put it up straight over him toward the sky and began walking matter of factly to the hotel. He went into the lobby and up to the desk with his hand above the head. We checked him in and got a key. We had the hotel guy get us some ice; and after getting the key, Chen Xiaowang said he would be ok and walked to his room and said he needed no help. That was an awkward start to a relationship that lead to around 15 or so seminars throughout the years. I felt bad because he was supposed to teach chin na in a couple of days, and I thought it may not be the best thing for his fingers to do chin na.

I don't know what he did in his room, but his fingers had lost any swelling, and he seemed as good as new the next morning. His chin na didn't seem to bother him a bit.

This nonchalant manner was consistent with him through all the years. He didn't act with the normal pride of a master. He would laugh at himself. When leading us through endless repetition of forms, he would sometimes lose his place. He would look over at me to see where I was going, and then he would not miss a beat. It didn't bother him that he was not a perfect person or master. I appreciated that from him.

I also appreciated that at the seminars, he tried teaching my students just as strongly and with great attention as he did with me or any of the instructors. It truly seemed like he wanted to get the most out of each student. There were times that I couldn't keep up, but he was easygoing, even though he worked each of us very hard.

It proved that he truly loved Tai Chi and was not just doing it for the money. He preferred to be understood clearly in all his teaching. Chen Xiaowang always asked me what I wanted him to teach at the seminars, and he always complied. As the years went on, we learned all the forms he teaches and most of the Chen weapons as well. Although we had learned the Chen Style from Gaofei and Uncle Chen, it was a different training. The legwork was tougher with each day, but Chen Xiaowang made you stay down more.

Master Chen came to us one year and was limping and bent over when getting out of the airplane. He said his back had been bothering him from all his travels. He said he needed a massage, so the next day Rick was able to get a masseuse to come over. Afterwards, Rick asked Chen Xiaowang if it was good, and he said the person had no power. So we ended up getting one or two more to come over, but he was not satisfied with their strength. Finally, he just got Rick to use the tip of his elbow while Chen Xiaowang told him what to do and where to go while bearing down. By the first day of the seminar week, he was fine and the limp was all gone.

Interestingly, we were learning Xinjia Yilu that week, and some of you will know that when you get to the basic punch in that form, Chen Xiaowang jumps about three or four times while doing arm movements. He jumps really high, pulling his knees up while at the peak of the jump. He did this into his 70's with us. Three or four times when he was teaching this form, we asked him if he could go over the handwork during the jumps. For some reason, he never would go slow enough so that we could pick up exactly what the movement was at one place.

So at the seminar with the bad back, we were at the very end of the last day, and Chen Xiaowang was asking for questions before we concluded the time together. Rick asked him about the same spot that we were unclear about. Chen Xiaowang starting saying, "Oh, you want to jump." Then he started asking who wanted to jump with him. So he would get a few people with him, and he would start jumping and demonstrating the movements that Rick was asking about. He seemed to enjoy this and would out jump everyone while doing it in repetition. Then he would stop and laugh a lot.

We then concluded the seminar, and he walked over to Rick and started guiding him over to the stage where he laid down and asked Rick to start digging that elbow into him again. So I was surprised that he was doing all that jumping that week with his back giving him some trouble. Most of the health issues he had were due to the thousands of miles he was stuck on a plane traveling. The first time he ever did that was the second or third year he came down. It was at Berry college, and again we were at the end of the seminar at 9pm, and one of the younger students asked him about the movement in Laojia that has the double jump kick. He said, "Oh, you want to jump. Who wants to jump with me." So a few tired folks came out to jump. He began doing the jump kick nonstop. It would be a right jump kick, but as his left foot came down, he continued with a left jump kick. He was quite an athlete; and even at that age, he jumped that night probably 30 straight times and was kicking way above his head. Then he stopped and laughed real big. It was one of the moments when you realized he was the best athlete in the room—and probably the oldest one.

I don't see Chen Xiaowang as much anymore since he has drastically reduced his traveling. He is set up well in Chen Village with a museum of his calligraphy and a new house built for him. I will always realize the he had a dramatic effect on my martial art and the understanding of internal training.

Bai Shufu Picture with Chen Xiaowang in 2006

CHAPTER 38
2006 - TRIP TO CHINA

CHEN XIAOWANG CAME up to me one time in Florida and asked me if I wanted to come to China and participate in an indoor disciple ceremony under him. I was caught by surprise. It was probably after about six years, and I told him that I was honored that he asked; but that I had to teach other arts in order to make a living and didn't want that to be a bad mark on him in any way.

He said that there was no problem, and he didn't care. I realized that his honor was not in the old traditional sense, but was because he wanted to honor all his hosts in the USA and throughout the world who put him up for these week-long visits.

Baishifu

The Chen Family had never really done this sort of thing in the past because they were all family. Everyone knew who the best ones were, and there was just no need for designation. But as the Chen teachers were trying to organize the new lives they had and to make a better business, many of them began to have ceremonies in China once a year. This was the first one that Chen Xiaowang held, and it was in March/April of 2006. There would be a ceremony, and then we would have a week of seminar teaching. There were about eight hosts in the US that went, and there would be about 70 in all that represented various parts of the world. Six students went with me to this event. This was my first trip to the mainland, and it was very exciting. We were just going to visit the Shaolin Temple, so there would not be a lot of sightseeing.

We had rain the first day, so we had to have class in a concrete building that was unfinished. The next day was the ceremony. I was obviously distracted, so it took a couple of days to settle down. The rest of the week we learned the Chen Style Double Saber form from Chen Xaiowang. Chen Xaiowang was a rock star in Chen Village. People were pulling on him from every direction—news media, villagers and not sure who else. We enjoyed the people in Chen Village as they were very friendly. The food in Chen Village was simple. It was not horrible, but not necessarily to western taste. After we were shown some places to have meals, we had some very delicious Chinese food. Chen Village was still pretty much a third world area at the time, but the government was coming in to make changes.

All the host from the US that were invited.

We made some friends on that trip. Some we would continue to communicate with for many years on Facebook or by email. Some of the other US hosts ended up coming to Florida for our Chen Xiaowang Seminar. We felt we were lucky because, for many years, Chen Xiaowang came to both Tennessee and Florida, so I would get him two weeks each year. I don't think anyone else had that situation. Also, most of the places just had him teach the seminar groups on Friday night and then two long sessions on Saturday and Sunday.

About the third year, he told me that he would prefer to have a five-day seminar, so that's what we did. We felt fortunate to get so much devoted time from him. Compared to going to China to study, it was much cheaper, and there was no comparison as to the attention you would get from him here. I also benefitted the first several years from private instruction throughout the week prior to the seminar days.

When we came back from China, we thought our sore legs would never be the same. It was good to make the trip. I had been to Taiwan, but never to the mainland. It was also good to see the countryside village and how things operated in the city. It was also good to be doing the Tai Chi with others in the city that had begun a tradition with a large extended family that practiced an art form which has lasted well over three hundred years.

In the village, you can practice on the concrete at the school or compound. You can also go down by the ditch (Chen Village Ditch) and practice on the ground, which feels like you are out of the city and alone in nature. You can visit the graveyard of the Chen Family and see all the stones and monuments erected for the famous Tai Chi masters in each generation. It is a good experience and now the only question remaining was... Would our legs ever be the same?

CHAPTER 39
INJURIES

I HAD BEEN fortunate throughout my life regarding injuries. Later in 2006 after the camp, I had my first knee injury. It was a little strange because I was becoming more and more strict on my posture with my knee consistently going into the right place more of the time.

However, the damage I had done in previous decades doing various things that affected my inner right knee made it so that it was just ready to pop one day. So I tore my inner right meniscus. After an MRI, the doctor said that since I taught professionally, he would normally go in and clean up the cartilage. Only ten percent of the cartilage in the knee has blood flow in it and can be restored. So the option was that after the swelling went down, there was no need to do surgery if I wasn't hurting. So I rehabbed myself, and it was pretty rapid. In just over a year, I regained everything I had in regard to movement and in terms of depth of posture.

This injury had a good side, since it made me even stricter about what my knees were doing all the time. So you see that the bad times have a positive aspect.

You have heard that when Bruce Lee was on his back in the hospital from an injury, it ended up being a time of growth for him mentally.

CHAPTER 40
2012 - TRIP TO CHINA

Earl Morgan - Maxie Green - Mark Yates - Joe Rea Phillips

SIX YEARS after the China trip, I had made a couple of decisions. I wanted to turn over the complete control of my seminars with Chen Xiaowang to Paul Vieira. Although we had a decent sized group for Chen Xiaowang through the years, I wanted him to have larger groups to teach. In the back of my mind, I was also aware that Chen Xiaowang wanted to quit traveling outside of China. He had already dropped South America that year. We had been spoiled for many years, but I knew that someone of his stature should probably be teaching larger groups. I knew that Paul was a great promoter and could make this event a lot bigger.

Figures of famous Chen Masters. Chen Wang Ting the founder.

The other thing was that there was another trip to China that Chen Xiaowang was pushing. I did not have so much an interest in going second time around, but I did want to see if Chen Xiaowang would allow some of my students to be inducted as indoor students as I had been. I wanted to offer this to people who were dedicated to the Chen Tai Chi and had also been supportive of all the years we had brought Chen Xiaowang to Florida and Tennessee. So I asked Earl Morgan, Joe Rea Phillips, Rick Lupe and a few more. I also wanted to recommend Paul Vieira since I had hoped he would take over the seminars in Florida.

So when he visited Florida, I was able to get CP Ong to help me present my request as clearly as possible to Chen Xiaowang. He was positive in his response. The only ones that were able to make the trip and do the ceremony were Joe Rea Phillips and Earl Morgan. Both had supported every seminar through the years. Neither Rick or Paul could go that year.

I was not planning to go, but some of the guys that were going wanted me to come along. A couple of them actually contributed money for me to go. So I went but tried to save money by not paying for the six-day seminar part. I thought I would just have fun taking pictures of Chen Village and getting to know more about the village.

It was kind of fun because the village had changed, and they had huge hotels and a Tai Chi stadium that was being built.

Tai Chi Statues and Museum in the Tai Chi Park

They had added a large Tai Chi Museum in the new Tai Chi Park. In the park was a huge concrete Yin/Yang Symbol that can be seen from pretty far up in an airplane. They also added some very nice large Tai Chi statues showing various postures. So while the guys were in their seminar, I was out and around the village taking pictures and getting to know the lay of the land. The people were very nice and friendly compared to the people in Beijing. It is sort of like the difference in the people in the urban areas of the US compared to the rural small cities, particularly down south.

One of the strangest things that happened on this trip was that, while in the village, I thought I saw Chen Quanzhong (Uncle Chen) get off of a bicycle and go into the compound where Chen Xiaoxing runs a large school. This is where I stayed during both trips since there are dorms available for housing.

I had to find out, so I ran and caught up with him as he was walking through the compound. We had spent some time together in the US. He taught me Cannon Fist form privately, but I didn't know if he would recognize me; he looked exactly like I remembered him. He stopped walking a few moments as I tried to think of words or people that he would recognize to jog his memory. He was so gracious and kind, but I am pretty sure he did not know who I was. It is certainly possible that it was not Chen Quanzhong. He normally lives in Xian, which is a long ways away; and although he visits Chen Village sometimes, it is not often. Joe Rea Phillips also caught sight of him and thought it was he as well. I looked for him the rest of the day, intending to get several of the students to go up to him at once. But I didn't see him again.

On this trip, Joe Rea Phillips, Earl Morgan, Maxie Green and Mark Yates went along. It was a fun trip with those guys present. We also went to Shaolin Temple and were able to visit the Great Wall before returning to the States.

Large Yin Yang Symbol in Tai Chi Park

Chen Village was being transformed rapidly. There is a bright and a sad side to it. I love to see the village get money to improve the quality of life. At the same time, it is being transformed so much that it looks less and less like the farm village it used to be. People were moved out of residences in order to make room for the hotels, stadiums and parks. Since 2012, it has changed a lot more, and I'm not sure what the end game is. The government has its areas, such as the museum, park and stadium where they charge an admission fee for visitors to go in and enjoy. This money does not go to the Chen people but to the government, so you can see that on one hand, some people get the benefit of a higher standard of living with improved electricity and plumbing. On the other hand, some people and places are discarded, and it seems they are using the accomplishments of this Tai Chi family for their own benefit.

At this point in time (2022), it looks like Chen Xiaowang is finishing a nice home being built for him, as well as a museum for his calligraphy.

So Joe Rea Phillips and Earl Morgan got to do the indoor student ceremony, and I got a ton of pictures. It was a nice trip.

Tai Chi Statues

CHAPTER 41
CHEN BING

Chen Bing, nephew of Chen Xiaowang teaching Taiji Sword

AS OUR SEMINARS with Chen Xiaowang were coming to a close, we had been able to have a few sessions with his nephew, Chen Bing. Chen Bing was in his late 30's when we first made contact with him. So we picked up more and more seminars with him to the point that we had two weeks a year for a while. We ended up enjoying 12 or 13 weeks over several years with him. He definitely filled in the gap when Chen Xiaowang quit coming.

Chen Bing teaching the CBII Chattanooga Group

Chen Bing was very good and was maybe the nicest guy I was ever around from the Chen Family. He was quiet and did not speak as much English as Chen Xiaowang. He did speak some, and some of my students like Rick Lupe could communicate with him better than I. I think he could understand Rick's Ohioan English better than my Tennessee English. When we hosted Chen Bing for a week, he mostly stayed in his room and communicated via computer with his home. He was starting to travel more and more, and you could tell that he missed home and his family.

When he taught, he was all business and a great teacher. He was very relaxed, and that was one of his strong assets. He got better every year.

When we started having him in Tennessee, he stayed at Sam Locklear's house in Dalton, Georgia. He told us a few years later that it was one of his top two places to stay in the US. Sam has a beautiful lake at the foot of his backyard, and Chen Bing was excited about fishing, as he had not been able to do too much back in China. Sam even got an expert to come over to help him. The area was very peaceful, and he loved to stay there. He also loved the cooking of Sam's wife, Erico. She was an excellent cook, and Sam always invited us over one night during the seminar for dinner.

Chen Bing played a role in my Tai Chi development. With Chen Xiaowang, I had learned both his Laojia and Xinjia system along with the main weapons of Chen Tai Chi. My first priority was to be able to get the technical side of his system down before focusing more on the principles. I might should have done that in reverse, but I felt a time

crunch to collect the data before we lost our opportunity to study with him. In following Chen Xiaowang, there were always a few movements that were hard to follow and feel. I tried to duplicate what I saw, but I always knew I was missing something. There are a few of those movements in Xinjia Yilu.

When we started having Chen Bing, I wanted to play down the confusion between all the forms, as all the teachers do little things differently, even if they come from the same general line. So I decided to focus on Xinjia more when Chen Bing came. He taught us some of the weapons, but my concern was more with the main forms. I had learned Xinjia from Chen Xaiowang and wasn't sure at first what was going to be different.

Some of the moves that were hard for me in Xinjia were small movements that Chen Xiaowang would do so small that it was not easy to feel what was going on. After we had learned Chen Bing's method, we started having him just take movements and go deeper for us. He was willing to do that. So when we were learning the movements that I referred to in Xinjia, Chen Bing helped me focus on relaxing and breathing. His execution of the movement was much larger than Chen Xiaowang's. This large movement seemed very different, but I began to practice it and could feel how it was supposed to be internally and unitarily because the large relaxed movement was easier to feel.

Chen Bing seminar in South Florida

So after a while, I decided to go back and look at Chen Xiaowang doing these movements in his small method. As I looked and studied closer, I realized that it was the same movement Chen Bing was teaching us, only greatly reduced.

I was so thankful because without that training from Chen Bing, I would never have understood the connection between large and small movement.

Chen Bing had to stop traveling during covid, as did most of the Chen masters. I'm not sure what the future holds since it will depend on covid and the groups that want to bring him over. Chen Bing has two or three students in the US that are his students and dedicated to him. He seemed to favor us because of our connection to his Uncle Chen Xiaowang. I am sure he has to weigh how much time he wants to be gone and decide what are his most productive travels, etc. So I'm not sure of being able to host him for future seminars. But he was very generous with his teaching and knowledge, and I will always be very grateful for this.

I want to say that all the Chen Xiaowang seminars and Chen Bing seminars in South Florida were facilitated by a lot of help from Paul Vieira. Paul is an excellent martial artist that agreed to support the seminars with his students. I would not have had near as many seminars without his help.

PART FOUR
SENIOR LIFE

CHAPTER 42
TEACHING SENIORS

SO I WAS APPROACHING my 60's, and one of my students, Sachiko Khaw, was moving out of South Florida to Georgia; and she asked me if I wanted to take over her Senior Classes. I had taught some Seniors over the years at Broward General Hospital, but I had never taught classes comprised only of Seniors.

So I had a lot to learn, such as understanding what things needed to be adapted because of age or condition. There is also a mindset that occurs. Some seniors are well adjusted, and some live and talk only of their next doctor's appointment and the meds they are taking. Odds are that only 3-4 percent of the students will actually practice. So in choosing a class plan, you don't want to overwhelm everyone with data but teach something that will help them. If they start thinking it is good, they might do some of it at home.

Focal Point Pembroke Pines, FL Senior Class

After a few years, I began to realize that there were some things about teaching seniors that exceeded teaching the younger. In most of my martial teaching, I was teaching people how to protect themselves, as well as how to deliver destructive force and techniques. I don't have a problem with that if I am teaching good people—people who don't want to use martial arts in a wrong way.

With seniors I was learning how to focus more and more on improving their health. So it was very fulfilling to hear comments about how the exercises we did had helped them so much in their daily life functions. You definitely get the feeling that you are contributing to people's lives in a very positive way.

Seniors usually have more health concerns. Many are afraid of falling for good reason. Many have mental diseases starting to invade their life. So it has been an education for me, especially since I am a senior now. Being a senior and having had some health issues, I understand their position a lot more, particularly about all the doctor visits and the meds. One's worldview comes into play with this situation as well. I just don't want to spend 24/7 focused on healthcare and insurance. I realize that everyone's health is different, and I certainly want everyone to be as healthy as possible. Seniors need to exercise. They need to get their quads strong, which will cut down on falls quite a bit. Seniors need to work on various kinds of mobility. Some seniors would follow instructions in my classes and actually practice. It was rewarding to actually contribute to a healthy lifestyle and help keep people out of the hospital.

Many thanks to Sachiko Khaw for introducing me to this world of teaching the martial arts. It has been rewarding, and I have met a lot of nice people.

Focal Point Pembroke Pines, FL Senior Class

CHAPTER 43
2018 - NOW I'M A SENIOR, MORE ISSUES!

AROUND 2015 I began having a breakdown of my left hip. It was tolerable, but after about a year and a half, I went to the doctor and found out that it was osteoarthritis, which is a deterioration of the cartilage. It starts to move you toward bone on bone. The doctor said this type of arthritis is caused by genetics or trauma. I had no genetic history, so I figured it was all the falls on my hip and all the kicks that hit my hip since I was 13 finally taking its toll on me.

They always try to give you a cortisone shot which lasts people for different amounts of time. I got one and it was only effective for about five days. There was also a type of gene therapy available that was supposed to help replace the cartilage. It was very expensive, and the reviews were mixed.

The long term solution was a hip replacement, but I knew the surgery was too expensive. So in 2018, I turned 65 and was eligible for Medicare. I had been dealing with the hip for three years. The last year it got very difficult. I was still teaching, but it was affecting my movement more and more. I was thrilled to turn 65 more than I normally would have been.

Since it was bone on bone in the last 6 months, I learned some valuable things. When we sit down in the legs completely, the hip joint has a separation that keeps the bone on bone from touching, or at least it is reduced. So I could go from extreme pain to no pain by dropping into a deep root. This is great for a little bit, and then you realize what Uncle Chen used to say. He stated that if I do what I am suppose to do, I can't even finish my form; it is too difficult. So this was good and bad news.

So medicare started in July, and I was able to get the new hip in September of 2018. My wife told me that I went from an old man to a young man overnight. It is amazing what modern medicine can do in certain circumstances. Nothing could have gone better, and I was able to do some limited teaching in just over two weeks. It took about 6 months to get my stretch back, but I could do most everything else a few weeks after the surgery. I was told to try and not pound the hip. So while I know this thing can be very durable, you wouldn't want to fall on or get kicked in the hip. So this was my official transformation more to a coach.

It is 2022 and I just had my other hip replaced. I had the same good experience with the hip, but I also had complications due to the anesthesia they gave me. These secondary complications cleared up mostly at the seventh week and completely by the three- month mark. So I am grateful for modern science which has allowed me to extend my teaching career as well as my ability to practice the martial arts.

Health is valuable and has a great effect on us, but it is still not the most important thing in life. I say this because I continue to meet people who have had horrible health, sometimes their whole life, and have many reasons to be dismal. Instead, they are an inspiration because they have a worldview that is not based on themselves. It is based on their Creator whom they have chosen to have peace with in spite of the condition they are in. Some are in these conditions through no fault of their own. These people have had a profound effect on my thinking.

CHAPTER 44
HAPPY TRAILS

I REALLY DIDN'T PLAN to ride off into the sunset for CBII, so in 2019 I began to think about the CBII and what the future would be. I wanted to stay involved, but more as a consultant rather than the force pushing the CBII. We started this organization in 1981. Casey died in 1986, so I kept pushing it along; but it primarily consisted of my students. When I looked at the average age of the main teachers of CBII, they were all in their 60's. The younger instructors were few—like Cameron, Anthony, Bryan, Patrick and a few others. But I thought there was a legitimate chance this wonderful art might not make it into the next generation. Some younger ones really needed to get a vision for the future.

So we arranged a gathering at a nice location with cabins up in the northern mountains of Georgia and Tennessee. We had a couple dozen instructors and old timers there, and we had about four large houses/cabins where everyone was staying. We met at the largest one for our meetings.

The first day was sort of supposed to be a state of the union speech. I was going to recite the history of CBII and what all had happened. I was talking about the various curriculums and their development through the years. Finally, in the last session of the first day, I gave an appeal for the instructors who would be willing to commit to a strong effort to teach and get younger people involved in our art. At the end, there were lots of questions and opinions, and the opinions were swinging a direction that I didn't expect.

We had a student who had become instructor level in Chinese Boxing. Alan Baker was just under 50 years old and had spent his whole life since childhood studying and earning instructor levels in about 20 arts, including our core Chinese Boxing curriculum. He had also pursued the marketing side of the martial arts and had helped a few big-named martial artists to enhance their business plan using his methods.

Some of the instructors brought this up, and the final tally was to ask me to continue leading the CBII but to try Alan's method for a time. So we began the Chinese Boxing Instructors Association. This was to be an outreach, primarily thorough free social media, to develop a voice about what CBII was all about and how we were actively training instructors. We wanted to attract Commercial Schools that were looking for an additional program in their school. I had to go to work and develop a video archive for the internet since we would have a members only site from which one could study every aspect of the curriculum. I had to put together a curriculum with levels, and I doubled the CB Synthesis curriculum, putting it together with eight levels leading up to instructor level. Those that joined would also get three camps per year so that those studying by video could get together and be corrected and work toward instructor level to represent CBII and its methods. So from September to January I/we got busy putting this together, and CBIA officially started January 1, 2020.

We had two camps the first year and three in 2021. It was pretty bad timing because covid hit and the commercial schools to which we were trying to appeal were struggling, with many closing. So our membership was primarily the instructors we had, some of whom talked some of their instructors into joining. We ended up with around 30 members and instructors. In spite of the bad timing, it did bring a lot of our guys closer together and stimulated a lot of thought in the new curriculum.

In 2022 we added a second program to the mix—Internal martial arts. We have a three-level program that applies to all the internal arts, and then another five levels in the style of one's choosing. One can move into Chen Tai Chi, Yang Tai Chi, Pakua and Hsing-i.

The internal arts are practiced by many in the world, so they will last some generations into the future. The part that we play is in adding the martial method aspects which are unique to Chinese Boxing. The Chinese Boxing curriculum we call KAI SAI Chinese Boxing is unique, and this is what we want to keep going. The unique parts of this are applied to the application aspects of the Internal Arts, making them unique in application to others.

So we will continue for a while to push an uptick in our membership in order to try to improve the long-range health of the CBII Group.

So it was an unexpected ending to a nice weekend, and it set me out on a new project.

CHAPTER 45
THE CHALLENGES LEFT

AT THE MOMENT, I am involved heavily in pushing the CBII through the Chinese Boxing Instructors Association. So regardless of the outcome of this project, what are the challenges left for Chinese Boxing?

For some time I have been trying to get people comfortable with the direction of the Encounter. From entry to touch to finish, there is important footwork that must become comfortable, and there are more drills needed to emphasize good timing and to execute a Chinese Boxing finish. So teaching and creating drills to develop this is a challenge and priority in the coming years.

Secondly, in order to practice with a partner frequently, there has to be an intelligent method for working on the powerful aspects of the encounter in a safe way while imitating as closely as possible the energy of real fighting. This has always been a huge challenge. Without these things developed at a high level, the Chinese Boxing method will only be a theory on paper—not one that can be implemented.

I have always felt that the Kai Sai method could be implemented, but that one has to be driven and adaptive. Casey's method was highly dependent on strong projection. Other strengths can help one implement the method as well. The footwork and forward pressure can be learned by everyone. If you have this strong base, then you can adapt to things within the encounter by improving your skill sets.

PART FIVE
WORLD VIEW

CHAPTER 46
JOURNEY TO A BETTER WORLD VIEW

THIS CHAPTER IS MORE personal to my life and contains a look at my worldview. I know that many of you are already aware of my worldview. Even though it isn't supposed to be proper to speak of religion or politics, I want to speak of the most important things that exist in life. Religion is not what I am about per se, and politics are maddening. Worldview represents the lens through which I see everything. We all know that "religion" is full of hypocrisy because it is full of people. Politics are loaded with corruption because politics involve lots of people. I was inspired early on that there was a rational way to approach life; and if one could be objective and honest, then most things could be figured out. I was pretty off on that assumption as my honesty and objectivism were difficult to maintain. At least knowing that helped me in my search.

If I really wanted to know the truth, the truth would probably not be perfectly in line with my thinking. If I wanted to make God into the type of person that pleased me, then it was probably not going to be the true God of the universe, but only someone like me.

My journey in martial arts began in 1966. The entertainment field, which showed programs like Man from Uncle, Wild Wild West and Green Hornet, stirred my imagination in the martial art scene.

There were people on these shows that fought differently from the status quo. Of course I was looking at it from ignorant eyes, and my life was all about me; but it did capture my imagination.

When I began martial arts training, I was interested in the self-defense aspect. I had been attacked by a guy with a knife on my first day walking home from Junior High. After talking with my dad, he agreed to let me learn more about protecting myself. Self-defense interest didn't last too long because the school I was in focused on sparring and traveling to tournaments. In those days the rules called for light contact, but the reality was that it could turn into a very bloody fight. So preparation was intense, and I had to expect more than just a friendly afternoon sparring class at the kwoon. I never really enjoyed this part of the martial arts, but I was highly competitive and did pretty well. Winning a few trophies brings one to the false conclusion that you think you know self-defense. Again and often, the **truth** was what I wanted it to be rather than something that came about honestly through rational and objective thinking.

After a few years of this, I joined the Pailum Association and became interested in aspects other than sparring and trying to win trophies. I enjoyed learning the numerous forms from the different methods of Shaolin and the massive material of Chinese Hawaiian kempo techniques with the Chinese Okinawan Kempo. In fact, I began to document each move and motion of all these forms and techniques. I could memorize physical sequences pretty easily. It enabled me over time to write and produce films of this material, and I began to sell 8mm films and instruction manuals.

In 1976, my martial art world turned to a new direction. I had gone to Taiwan with the Pailum Association, and I remember going around Taiwan and doing demonstrations with the Pailum group. At one place, I was actually demonstrating a form for some of the leaders of the Republic of China (Taiwan) Congress in the main auditorium of their Congressional Hall.

Believing myself to be very important, I'll never forget a gentleman that stepped up to me who could speak English. Turns out he was some kind of well known teacher who was in charge of the bodyguards for some of the political leaders in Taiwan. I arrogantly thought he was about to compliment my performance. I'll never forget what he said. He told me that I had some potential, but I would never reach it if I didn't find a real teacher. He did not know my history or the fact that even on that trip I was deciding to leave my present teacher. My teacher had a lot of knowledge and could fight, etc., but I had discovered many things in the organization that I could not be proud of and were questionable to anyone with a moral conscious. I knew that I needed to leave, but I had no idea where or to whom I could go in order to get a better education. Just shows how blind we can be at various points of our life. **Truth** was not going to come from the wrong teacher.

It was at that time that I became Mr. Christopher Casey's student. His passion in the study of martial arts was something I had never really considered. I naively thought at the time that my sparring skills could take care of me in a real fighting situation. In my first lesson with him as a private student, he showed me that he could control my energy and tie me up so that I would be dead in a real fight. While I was not fighting to destroy him, I was doing my best not to be controlled; and he was doing things I had never felt in combat. This inspired a completely new direction of thinking about the things I had learned and done up to then. Having experienced his skill, I could not deny that it existed; I just didn't understand it or how I could learn it.

Behind the scenes, Mr Casey was a philosopher. Due to his critical thinking skills, he approached the study of martial art much more rationally than I had ever done. But to have a clear purpose of the best way to fight realistically and not within any rules changed the landscape. Everything upon which I had based **truth** in the past was shown to have faulty premises and foundations. It was because I didn't understand realistic fighting. His approach to all this was twofold. Most of it was rational and very scientific, desiring high percentage results. Since it was real fighting, you did not have the luxury of making many mistakes and needed to learn to fight effectively and efficiently to the end. The other side of his approach was a little abstract, but no less effective. It was a little harder to grasp. It involved Mind Hit technique in fighting and energy touch skill. The mind study was not a hocus-pocus teaching, but actually involved steps you could achieve though practice. The energy touch skills were taught by most of his masters, using the dueling skills of Chi Sao, push hands and joint hands in order to control someone on contact. The nerves throughout the body had to be taught in the right way to respond to different stimuli. This could not happen using only rational decision making. Beginning with rational decision making, you could train your body to react in the right way with a lot of practice. These things were not easy, but over time you could experience progress.

The duels could also take you off-track easily, as they could almost become a game in itself, distracting one from staying focused on how this would apply in a realistic fight. So with Mr. Casey's thinking method, he was able to change the course of my outlook. Training for the realistic was the challenge, as you can only lose once in a realistic fight to the death. So using safety precautions without watering down the things you do destructively was the biggest problem and challenge.

Casey's study of philosophy led him to a worldview of agnosticism. An agnostic philosophy means that one does not know for sure the **truth** about something. For example, when one wants to decide if there is a God or not, it is not a yes or no answer. It is a belief that is founded on looking at the evidence and deciding one cannot know for sure. Mr. Casey decided that all he could count on in his life was the study of energy. The rest was unknown. As I learned things, I discovered that this decision was also a distraction when it came to the realistic life and death expectations that we all experience as humans. There are sincere agnostics that are searching, and there are others who are not searching; so basically they are atheist. Most philosophers see a problem with the atheism argument and position because to prove there is not a God is beyond their ability since there is so much knowledge about the universe that is yet unknown.

Mr. Casey and I had a few conversations about worldview. Surprisingly, he gave my position, which could be called reasonable faith, some respect.

The biggest question one faces in life is if there is a God or not. To decide whether there was a creator or whether this all happened by chance is the biggest decision. Regardless of what you decide, it will change the trajectory of everything in your life, just like a fork in the road sends you in two different directions. The lens you look through to interpret the world will be based on your answer to this question. The search and answer to this may take some time. If God is for real, what kind of God is He? What is His nature? To create all that we see, He has to be a God with immense power. To hold everything in place with the changes that occur would take power that is unimaginable. Since He created creatures that can think and have emotions, He must have some of these characteristics as well. But since we see injustice in the world, how could He be a good God and allow for these things?

There are many academic arguments for the existence of God. The moral argument is sometimes expressed like this. How does one differentiate between right and wrong? If there is good, then there has to be evil. If there is a right and wrong, there must be a moral law that determines this. If there is a moral law, then there must be a moral lawgiver. The option to this thinking is that all your ideas come from genetics or your environment. How can genetics and a soulless environment have any morality?

All of these are very difficult topics to tackle. What options do we have other than that there is a God. The option to God is really a world that appears cruel at times and has no justice and meaning. If it has no meaning, then what is the purpose of following any law? The atheist will say there are little meanings that make life worth living; but in the broad spectrum of space and time, all these little meanings will vanish in just a short time. They will not last, and no one will remember any of it after a short period of time. Frankly, this direction is unlivable to me. There is no hope, no meaning and no real purpose. If there is not someone who can make all things **just** in the end, this life is unlivable.

In the search for ***truth***, there are just a few large categories. One view is that there is a creator being, God. He created everything and is active, although partially hidden in that He has no physical form in the world today. This is called Theism.

Secondly, there is a worldview called Deism. It believes that a superior power created everything. But this power is aloof and does not enter into space and time to interfere with what he created. One is sort of on his own.

Thirdly, there is the worldview of Materialism or Naturalism. This is the view held by the majority of academics and scientists in the world. There is still a respectable number who don't hold it, but the majority fall into that category. Materialism and Naturalism is generally atheistic and states that all that exists in this universe is matter and energy. There is no creator, no afterlife, no supernatural. This view cannot explain where the world comes from. They have many theories but have yet to come up with one that turns inorganic into organic or turns matter into consciousness. That is a great divide that has never been crossed. They believe all your thoughts and mind activity are only a physical brain with matter that is determined. There is no soul or spirit. These are very difficult claims to prove. If one comes to this conclusion, then life is determined. If we are just a result of DNA fulfilling its course, then our lives are determined and no one actually has free will.

Finally, there is Pantheism. Pantheism encompasses a lot of the belief systems in Asia, such as Buddhism, Hinduism and New Age. This system has no creator but believes that we are all part of "the one." Usually, these systems believe in reincarnation. You can never know for sure that you can achieve enlightenment. You will come back as something lower or higher from your present existence based on whether you lived a good or bad life. It is a belief that is very relative. On the surface it is very relaxed and laid back. **_Truth_** depends on the person. There is your **_truth_** and there is my **_truth_**. There is no such thing as absolute truth. It is relative. Even the statement "There is no truth" is an absolute statement that contradicts the point being made. To me it has many issues, but it is often linked to many martial arts.

Theism, Deism, Materialism and Pantheism are the four major categories of worldview. There are hundreds of belief systems, but they will generally fall into one of the four. Let's look again at the first one. In the area of Theism, there are three options that are well known—Judaism, Christianity and Islam. To me, Islam can be eliminated just by learning the history of Mohammed. When Mohammed was able to get weapons, he spent over ten years taking over Arabia. He took small bands of fighters with him and attacked villages, seizing the women and cutting the heads off of all the males he could. There are countless wonderful people and families that think Islam is peaceful. The issue is exposed when their special scriptures (the Koran) are read. In the first half of his career, Mohammed did have teachings of peace in Islam that showed friendship toward the Jews and Christians. In the second half of his career, however, it was just totally brutal, and he destroyed many lives. In the book itself, one can see the verses that explain this attitude. He did not claim to be God, and he was unable to perform miracles other than how he claimed to have received the Koran. So this seems an unlikely candidate for the ultimate **_truth_**.

Judaism was unique as a mono-God system way back in history, while other civilizations were multi-god cultures. The Old Testament Law claimed to have come from God, and the full Old Testament also included the History books, Poetry Books and the Prophets. These books speak of God's promises to the people of Israel and their struggle to follow God. In the end, the Jewish people were scattered all across the world, and we see today a movement of millions of Jews making their way back to their homeland, the nation of Israel. The scriptures also prophesy that in the end times, the Jews will come back to their God, and things do look to be going that direction.

Christianity embraces Judaism as part of Christianity. Christians believe in the God of the Old Testament. They believe that Jesus, who was a teacher and healer, was in fact the Son of God or God in the flesh who had come to earth to fulfill the promises of God in the Old Testament. When the Jews were scattered, they could not worship in their temple and perform the required sacrifices of animals for their sins. Christians believe Jesus to be the final sacrifice who gave up His life to pay for the sins of the entire world. The Jews in general rejected this message. They were looking for a Messiah that would take over Rome and set the world right. According to Christians, Jesus was the Messiah; but as predicted in the Old Testament, He (Jesus) would be rejected initially. It was because His purpose in coming the first time was to become a sacrifice for the sins of the world. The religion of Judaism used animal sacrifices to atone for their individual sins. They had to do this over and over again. Man is not perfect, so this was an endless cycle.

In Christianity, it is believed that Jesus became the final sacrifice, the once and for all sacrifice for man's sin. The sacrificial system found fulfillment in the coming of Jesus and His death on the cross. Although the Christian church was started by Jews, the bulk of the Jews rejected it. However, the Gentiles started believing the gospel that was proclaimed by the Jewish followers of Christ.

There are some amazing facts about the resurrection of Jesus from the dead that argue for the truth of Christianity. Nearly all of the original disciples of Christ willingly gave up their lives and were martyred for their faith. There is no doubt that these men along with many others were convinced of Christ's resurrection and were willing to give up everything for it. The spread of Christianity had amazing rapid growth even when people were being persecuted for their faith. In around 300 years, it had become the official religion of the Roman Empire.

Of course, as the church got big, it was corrupted as it strayed from the teachings of Christ. But the Old Testament and the New Testament spoke and prophesied of the return of Christ to set up a Kingdom toward the end of time. The teachings have amazing accuracy as we look at present world events as they line up for the end times spoken of in the Old and New Testaments.

I realize that if one believes in God, it is a big leap from that to Christianity. But as I study the options, this one makes the most sense to me. All religions of the world have spokesmen that tell you the things that you have to do in order to be on the right path for ***truth***. Christianity introduces Jesus as the One that did everything for us; and if we accept His offering by faith, we become part of His family for eternity. None of the other religious leaders ever claimed to be God. Jesus did. All other religions have a list of things you must accomplish to find the ***truth***. Christianity claims that Jesus is the ***truth***, and you cannot do anything to earn it—it only requires belief. So if one understands what Christ did and sincerely accepts by faith to follow His teachings and do good works, he is less likely to be hypocritical. But the things that man can do and the ceremonies and requirements get you nowhere. It is easy to see where the churches went wrong when they started providing ways to pay for sins, etc. That is a total corruption of all that Jesus taught.

Accepting Christ is a step down the road. So one must first come to the belief that God exists. This is a huge decision that splits your future into two very opposing directions. Your life is given to the Creator if you truly acknowledge Him as God and you want to learn what He is like. Or the other option is that there is no God, no purpose, no meaning, no real right or wrong and no hope for eternity. It means a life of determinism with no real freedom to choose. When you don't have a soul or spirit and only have a brain, science indicates that the decisions you make are programed by the influence of your genetics and environment. How can you trust your thinking if it is determined and this conclusion if it was just a part of natural selection and random chance. We should not talk about ultimate ***truth*** claims because it might offend someone.

Unfortunately, most people float through life and never try to answer this most important question. They just live and let live. They believe that their destiny is not affected by what they believe. Often, circumstances or big trouble in life will cause one to confront this important topic, but many just ignore it their whole life.

In the martial arts, what I found as the best approach to the most serious questions in combat involved a rational approach. This makes science part of the equation. But there is a subjective and less objective side which involves touch and feeling and cannot be so easily quantified through science. In worldview and ultimate ***truth*** concerns, belief, faith and confidence are what hold these two sides together—not belief in myth, but reasonable faith in the reality of the evidence of God and His plan.

In the search for truth in the real world, there is a science and logic to understand. God gave us logic and gave us the world to discover. In the scriptures, it is declared that he that comes to God must *believe* that He is and that He is a rewarder of those who seek Him.

In Christianity, God demands faith, but not unreasonable faith, rather reasonable faith based on research, logic and critical thinking. But in the end, He wants you to take a step of faith and believe. One cannot earn this. Christianity answers a lot of questions about the world in which we live. For example, we see all the injustice and imperfection in both nature and in the world of people, and we wonder how God can permit these things and be a God that is good. The scriptures teach that sin entered the world near the beginning of creation because God gave humans a free will to make choices. It always comes down to whether we want to live our own life, or do we believe that the God who created us may have something better if we follow His direction. Sin explains all the imperfection and injustice in the world. But God would not be worth seeking if He didn't provide an answer to the problem of sin and injustice.

The good news of Christ is His great love for each person that was demonstrated when He gave Himself up on the cross to take the judgment for our sins. This is the redemption that God has provided for each person.

He lived the perfect sinless life that we could not live, and He died the death that paid for sin that we could not accomplish.

There are many questions and things that bother people as they think about these matters. I know that to think about the possibility that there is a God is a very important question that deserves attention and study from an open honest heart.

If you would like any dialogue or discussion on these things, please feel free to contact me.

APPENDIX A - CASEY STORIES

I wanted to include the chapter I wrote in "the boxing" book to further give stories about my teacher Christopher Casey and some of the training with him.

The Story of a Gift
by James Cravens

My story begins in about 1973. I had been in the martial arts fourteen years studying different forms of karate, tang soo do, ju jitsu, Shaolin and was in about the fifth year of a nine year period in which I was a member of the Pailum Association. Essentially this was a group who's curriculum consisted of what Daniel Pai taught as well as the combined knowledge of everyone that joined or participated with the Pailum organization.

I only visited with Mr. Pai in Hartford, CT in the summers and whenever I met him at tournaments. I was satisfied at the time with my training as Mr. Pai was a talented athlete, strong, fast and tough martial artist He taught me never to give up and how to raise my intensity to whatever it took to accomplish the goal. At 21 years old I still admired him a great deal.

I was at home one Saturday morning and I received a call from a former instructor who told me that he was with a man who was asking him a lot of questions about Pailum Kung Fu and wanted him to show all he could about the style. This former instructor did not know much about Pailum, because he did not continue to study the martial arts formally and since I knew more about this topic, he asked for my help with this "visitor."

When I arrived, I saw a short man about five foot six or seven and about 175 pounds He didn't look very special and so I was introduced to Mr. Christopher Casey who told me he was researching Pailum Kung Fu and asked me if I could show him any Pailum Kung Fu and if so, would I mind if he recorded it on film I enjoyed showing off so I demonstrated a short Shaolin type form that I had learned from Mr. Pai. After I finished, Mr. Casey thanked me and asked whether I would show anything additional. My former instructor piped in saying that he should go study this form and then come back for more. I believe that Mr. Casey was offended by the response of my former instructor and so Mr. Casey and my former instructor said their goodbye's.

I stayed and talked to Mr. Casey and he asked me if I would mind showing him more of my "Pailum Training." I loved to show off so I proceeded to show him everything I knew and I suppose simultaneously everything I didn't know. He was extremely grateful and then took me out to eat where we had a long discussion.

This was my initial meeting with Mr. Casey. As the months passed he would call me and ask many questions about how my training was going as well as the general direction of my life. I quickly realized that this man was extremely bright and knowledgeable about the martial arts. He told me I was welcome to come train with his group at Georgia Tech anytime. I decided to ask Mr. Pai about him as I was a loyal student and would never study from another without permission. Mr. Pai surprised me by saying that I should learn all I could from that man, because he knew a lot. That's all I needed and I was to begin going down to Atlanta from Chattanooga for the next four years to study.

During this time Mr. Casey would teach me Shaolin form, Chinese Hawaiian Kempo from James Mitose-Thomas Young lineage, Kodakan Jujitsu from the Okazaki/Lindsay lineage, Chinese Okinawan Kempo, Shorinryu and Uichiryu Karate, and a variety of chin na methods.

My impression of Mr. Casey during these years was that he was probably the smartest person I had ever met in the martial arts, and he was very intense as he would demonstrate application etc. I never sparred with him or watched him spar with anyone. Therefore, while I thought he was light years ahead in knowledge, I privately thought I could whip him in a real fight. I didn't care, I reasoned, because I was studying to increase my knowledge, and after all, Pailum was where my loyalty resided. I was surely glad Mr. Pai encouraged me to study with Mr. Casey.

Mr. Casey would call me from time to time, and sometimes things he would say would bother me because he could not understand the actions of the Pailum organization. While arguing for my group, I had to admit that he was making points that were bothering me, but I was unwilling to face.

Meanwhile, a big trip to China was planned for July of 1976 with Mr. Pai and the Pailum organization. This was a very exciting expectation and I and three of my students were looking forward to the trip. The trip is an entire book by itself, but without going into detail, there were things that happened that forced me to reconsider my future with this organization. I decided to resign my position with the organization. At the time it was a very difficult decision even though it was probably something I should have done a lot sooner. It is not my point to belittle this group. It is only that one has to become honest and realistic about life goals and life messages that one wants to project. It had become apparent that my goals and messages had become very different from those of the Pailum organization.

The trip was a long one lasting through about half the summer. I knew a couple weeks before the end that I would be leaving this group. I began to agonize over what I would do and where I would go. At the time I thought Mr. Pai was the ultimate as a martial artist. Everything available in the world became a distant second. My mind finally returned to Mr. Casey and the knowledge that I knew he had. I felt at the time that I was a great fighter (I'm sure you have noticed my humility), but I still knew that I didn't know a lot of things. Therefore, while in Japan the last couple of weeks on our trip, I decided to write to Mr. Casey. I explained to him my situation and asked to become a formal student. Since I mailed it to him, I didn't know an answer for a couple of weeks. When I arrived in the states, I had an audio tape and letter waiting on me. He graciously accepted me as a student, and the audio tape was my first lesson.

I remember in that first lesson, which was an hour and a half lecture, that he told me that some people may be satisfied with their fishing hole because they don't know what else there is, but if one was taken out of the hole into the bay and eventually into the ocean the wonders awaiting would be unbelievable. Early on I guess he was trying to form an attitude that would become core in the training of Kai Sai Kung Fu. One must have no limit if he wants to expand and grow. One must be open and willing to be a student for growth to occur. I have met many a martial artist through the years that might have known a lot, been smart and may have been skilled who were closed minded and had no possible way to grow and learn.

Although I was all set to learn, it would not be easy as in the next five years, Mr. Casey would live in Miami, New Orleans, Seattle, and Hannover, West Germany. He climbed the corporate world of insurance and eventually a German company (Hannover Rhea) bought his expertise to bring them into the arena of international reinsurance so they could compete with Lloyds of London. During this time, my lessons were few (about four sessions a year) but packed with principle and technique, all I could hold and even practice for the next three months. We had lessons in motel rooms or anywhere that we could connect based primarily on his travels around the country. He called fre- quently which was like having a lesson in itself. He would usually talk for an hour and it would be almost all martial art and philosophy. Even at a distance it seemed as if I had a private tutor in my ear at all times. Having good students to help me learn was also a great advantage in developing this particular art.

During this time, I primarily studied Wing Chun and Wa Lu. There were other things as well, but these were the major things during this time period. At the end of this period as Mr. Casey was making a transfer to set up a subsidiary of the German company based in Stanford, Connecticut, we began another period in which he taught me marathons of technique. This came as a SAS-G curriculum (Special Action Service Group) which taught secret service training involving empty hand, vital point, knife and cane or stick work. Secondly it came in the form of the original Kai Sai Boards. Both of these curriculums evolved because of discussions with Mr. Casey concerning certain problems and desires involving my school and students. I was still teaching Kempo to beginners and waiting for students to advance before taking them into Chinese Boxing. I would tell him that I wished I could teach Chinese Boxing to people from day one. He responded with a curriculum he put together that would both have the flavor of realistic Chinese Boxing, yet be terribly interesting and simple enough to learn for the beginner. This SAS-G curriculum was his answer.

Also, during this time Mr. Casey began to introduce me to several other areas of Chinese Boxing. I would come back from Connecticut with some new area each time and then my students would want to learn the new "stuff." After a while, it became discouraging, because they were not developing high skill since they were jumping around to different arts etc. As I told Mr. Cascy the problem, he responded by developing the Kai Sai Boards. He got the idea from his study of Kodakan Jujitsu in Hawaii. Henry Okazaki had boards (long vertical ones) in his dojo listing the techniques of jujitsu in different categories. Mr. Casey chose ten categories and put twenty-five items on each category. He felt that the boards would draw techniques from the many styles that he had learned, and of course the principles of Chinese Boxing would be the foundation for any of these techniques. That way one could be using the "best" from many styles and not be floating between curriculums. He did believe that one should have one internal form to practice in order to be complete. Actually this idea has spawned an evolution of curriculums which now we call the Core Curriculum of Chinese Boxing Synthesis.

Mr. Casey obtained another student in Germany who was very special. His name is Manfred Steiner. Manfred was a great athlete and was a long time martial artist and champion in judo and Kiokashinkai Karate. Manfred studied just under two years while Mr. Casey was in Germany. He studied a lot as he could meet with Mr. Casey almost daily. Mr. Casey arranged a trip for Manfred to come to the U. S. and Manfred helped train me in Wing Chun and JKD for about three weeks. This was most helpful. After meeting Manfred it was hard to imagine anything or anyone who could handle this great fighter. Mr. Casey had no problem and that was why Manfred was interested in Casey.

About 1981 Mr. Casey moved back to the United States and the next five years was the time that I was able to have my best training with Mr. Casey. Since I had a regular seminar schedule in the Northeast US, it was very convenient to schedule stays with Mr. Casey during this period. Mr. Casey wanted to begin to teach the internal arts. He had taught me numerous curriculums and styles at this time, but now told me that I had learned much, but was still lacking in serious Chinese Boxing skill. Being a proud person, I was offended as usual, but as usual, he was right. He began to teach Pakua. He felt that it would match some of my natural abilities such as footwork. He did not teach me fast and furious as before, because he was trying to begin to teach me rooting, body state, and the principles that make a difference. He would not let me learn more curriculum unless I could maintain the root and body state that he expected. For someone who loved to transfer data on a fast modem this was like having a 600 speed modem today. But, it was necessary because although I thought

I knew what I was doing, I didn't and sometimes one needs a stern wake up call.

While Pakua remained the emphasis of my training he also taught some Hsing-i, shuai chaio, Tai Chi, and Fukien White Crane during the final six years. Mr. Casey died on December 13, 1986 and the last summer he quit his job and moved to Atlanta for a sabbatical. I didn't get to see Mr. Casey much during this period although we talked on the phone almost nightly. About ten of my students went weekly for ten weeks to study Saturday afternoons with Mr. Casey. This became a wonderful honor for many of my students who got to know this great martial artist for a little while and be participants in the vision of the great art of Chinese Boxing

IN A DIFFERENT LEAGUE

I have spoken about Mr. Casey and his background in my book on Chinese Boxing, but sometimes I marvel that I ever ended up connected to him. I am a bit average in many ways, but Mr. Casey was a gifted individual. He was from a family of gifted intellectuals. He could sit and talk about practically any subject with amazing knowledge. When he first invited me to come down to his apartment in Atlanta about 1973 I remember coming in and sitting down on the couch in his living room. On the coffee table was an unabridged dictionary that seemed to be about a foot thick. He saw me looking at it, and he told me to go ahead and pick out any obscure word. I did and he gave nearly a word for word definition. He told me to continue, and I must have done this another five times when I finally told him that I understood his point. He told me that he had something like a photographic memory and that he could remember about 98% of everything he read. He said he remembered things he didn't want to remember. After being with him for many years he continued to prove not only a high intelligence, but a very high gift in creativity as well.

The odds of me hooking up with someone like this are of course very small. If I sat and talked with Mr. Casey about practically anything, I would be truly in another league, but as destiny would play out, he had a 30 year love affair with the martial arts and his path crossed mine on that Saturday morning. For some strange reason he stayed in contact until the day that I became a formal student. Basically these things cannot be explained and as a Christian I don't say it was luck, but it was definitely a gift from above.

A BIG FIRST LESSON

After becoming a formal student, my first physical lesson with Mr. Casey was truly one to remember. You may remember that even though I had learned Kempo and Shaolin and chin na etc. from Mr. Casey during the years I had been in the Pailum organization, we had never done any free style duel or sparring. I was satisfied to study with Mr. Casey because I knew he could teach me things, but I still thought I could whip him.

A few months earlier he came up to see me fight in a tournament in Chattanooga. I had a good day and won the tournament. He didn't say anything much to me that day. Now, I was his student and I thought we would continue learning some topic that we had worked on before. After arriving at his house, he took me to where we would work out and asked me whether I wanted to spar. I thought to myself that I really didn't want an incident or to make him look bad. Mr. Casey always seemed in control when he was showing a technique, but he was in many ways awkward and you just couldn't believe that he could do well if we squared off to fight.

As we began to spar, I determined that I would just cover up and play defense and not take the chance of making him look bad. He moved around carefully for a moment and then attacked me. I covered up thinking I was on balance. The next thing I knew, I was taken down and he had me tied up in a ridiculous position where I was helpless. Well, this was a shock. The problem was, I expected him to get up and let me get up so we could try again. He held that position for what seemed like forever. It was probably only a minute and a half, but it seemed as though it were endless. Finally, he got up and went over to his chair and sat down. I looked at him with a puzzled look after standing and he looked back with a blank look. He finally spoke and asked me what I thought. I said, "Aren't we going to continue? He said "OK." He then got up and we began again. This time I would pay attention and although I didn't want to hurt him, I wasn't going to let the man walk in and do that to me again. Well, the same basic thing happened again. The first few times I kept thinking that I would make an adjustment and would prevent it from happening. Well to end a long story quick, he must have done the same thing to me at least twenty times. Finally he noticed my utter shock and asked me if a point had been made. I said yes, and finally he sat down. He asked me whether I was surprised by what had happened and I confirmed his suspicion.

He then began to ask me why I didn't punch him as I had punched everyone at the tournament he had watched. I told him I didn't seem to have the opportunity. He just smiled and shook his head. I asked him why he held me down so long. Then came the lesson: You have a dangerous idea that a fight consists of sharing a few blows with someone. You recklessly turn your back, and you have no idea how to stop a committed attack. Your tournament fighting has trained you to do things that are very risky in real fighting. Chinese Boxing is another world from what you are use to and I was holding you down for so long so that you would think about the fact that you were dead. You had made one mistake in the encounter, and you were dead. You can't get up and try again; you are dead. I was hoping you would think about this. Wow! Had I been introduced to Chinese Boxing or what? Though I was a bit battered that day I was elated. Why? Well, not only did my teacher know more than I, but he could whip me too. What could be better?

STOPPING JUST BEFORE MENTAL DESTRUCTION

On the same visit that the above story took place, I was about to get the mental version of what had happened physically the day before. I was sitting in Mr. Casey's living room with Mr. Casey and his wife Victoria. We were talking, and suddenly Mr. Casey was asking me what my philosophy of life was and what I believed. I am a Christian and that of course was quite different from Mr. Casey's beliefs. I began to tell him my beliefs and like a person who was a skilled lawyer Mr. Casey began to question and attack my every statement as if he were in mortal combat and going for the kill. I was definitely under attack, but I was actually enjoying the challenge to express my beliefs. The problem was that I was not doing a good job against this master philosopher. During this discussion I noticed that Mr. Casey's wife became very uncomfortable and would leave the room for a while and then return.

At one point all of a sudden, Mr. Casey quit the discussion and said, "Jim, I don't agree with your position but I respect your position because you have faith and I believe that the most important thing is that you possess that strong conviction. You do have a problem however, that you may be able to solve. You cannot adequately explain your position. You need to communicate your ideas with more skill. This is also "the Boxing." I never forgot the impact of this lesson and I did strive to improve my communication skills. After some time went by and I was much closer to Mr. Casey, his wife told me that she had witnessed many people sit with Mr. Casey and discuss their philosophy as we had done that early time of my training. She told me that she had seen many a student run out of their house. They would leave from panic, anger, inability to cope with the pressure Mr. Casey would apply. Most people do not know what they really believe nor can they defend their beliefs against a master lawyer. Mrs. Casey told me that the day that he had done this with me he suddenly quit. She had never seen him quit with anyone but would continue until a person cracked or ran out of the house in anger. She could not stand it when he would do this so she would leave the room. When she noticed that he stopped she was shocked as she had never seen him stop before. After I left that day, she asked him why he had stopped. He told her that he just realized that he was using his talents for destructive purposes and that he should change and use his talents for positive endeavors. She said that he never did such a thing again. I don't believe I had anything to do with this, but again the power above permitted me to participate in an interesting synchronistic event and turning point in the life of Christopher Casey.

On a continuing note, Mr. Casey would ask me occasionally some questions about Christianity. He told me he had trouble relating to Christianity. He seemed surprised at times at the answers I would give. As you may remember, Mr. Casey had read the Bible and probably remembered 98% of what he had read. He seemed to only have the Catholic position on matters of Christianity. Some of his own personal interpretations of Bible events or stories were at the least very bizarre. I think the Protestant view of things took him by surprise since his education of Christianity had been limited to the Catholic position.

At one point years later, he was evaluating how he thought I would fare against another martial artist in an all out fight. He said that the other person probably would defeat me on paper, but he thought I still held the advantage and would win because I had a strong faith which made this life only a temporary point and that I did not fear death as the other person did. He believed that this difference would allow me to relax more and therefore make up the difference. I don't mention this to brag about myself After all, Christians believe that their honored position in Christ is all because of grace (unmerited favor). I do mention it in order to give you different insights to my teacher's ideas and thoughts. It is certainly for you to determine the value of this dialogue.

CHI SAO LESSONS

During my best years of study, I would often visit Mr. Casey in Stanford for three to ten days. The first day was usually dramatic. I think he orchestrated a very special first day on most visits. Mr. Casey was a special kind of teacher. He would first get one's complete attention and teach in a way that you would have to figure out the lesson for days and weeks ahead. He demanded a thinker. Otherwise, you would think the man was crazy at times.

My first chi sao lesson was a case in point. He told me after arriving and having cookies and tea, that he was going to teach me chi sao. He began by getting me to put my right arm in a bong sao position. He put his left arm and fist in a vertical punch position touching my bong sao. He told me that he was going to try and punch my chest on center and it was my job to deflect and prevent him from punching the center chest. He proceeded to pound my chest about thirty times in a row. I knew what he was going to do, but no matter how I moved he hit me in the sternum in the same place. Finally, he threw up his hands and exclaimed that I knew nothing about holding center. I told him that I knew that and that is why I was there to learn. He looked frustrated and went upstairs for the rest of the day. The rest of the trip he didn't even talk about chi sao and other things were practiced and taught.

I was going crazy wanting to know what I needed to do to learn how to hold center. I would ask him questions, but he diverted the conversation to other topics. Well, I would figure it out, so I went back home and grabbed a poor student. I put his arm in a bong sao, and now I was going to pound his chest. After getting in a couple of cheap shots, my student began to deflect some of my punches. Why couldn't I deflect Mr. Casey's punches? Over much practice and discussion and formal training in chi sao, I began to learn how Mr. Casey read my energy that day and knew everything about how I would respond and therefore could place his punch on the same target no matter how hard I tried to prevent it. Yes, learning to hold center was a great lesson. One that I not only could not forget, but just had to have the answer to the puzzle. If he simply had told me, I might not have valued the lesson. Mr. Casey would eventually answer your questions, but he wanted you to go through the thinking process so that you would understand fully on your own and without being spoon fed. As in the death of Henry Okazaki, most of the Black Belt instructors would spend their time together arguing about how Mr. Okazaki taught a particular technique. There were a few (Wally Jay to name one) who could think for himself and pursued the truth rather than the technique.

TOO MUCH TECHNIQUE AND NO SKILL

During the first two or three years as an official student of Mr. Casey, he would call me before I would visit him and he would ask me what I wanted to learn. Imagine that, like a kid in a candy store I could ask for anything. Was this heaven or what? Sometimes you get what you ask for and I was asking for this and that. In a three year period I learned the Kai Sai Board curriculum, the Wa Lu curriculum, some of the Wing Chun curriculum, the Special Action Service Group Curriculum. Before becoming an official student.

I learned the entire 286 techniques from Chinese Hawaiian Kempo as well as numerous Shaolin forms and techniques. I was "in my mind" growing extremely knowledgeable and certainly I was becoming better and better.

Mr. Casey took about all he could and finally one day I arrived at his place and he didn't ask me what I wanted. I had my wish list ready, but after watching me do some form he started to discuss my progress. He said that while the marathons of technique learning was interesting year after year, I was getting no better and my skills were not improving. He went on to say that having knowledge without energy is empty and worthless. He said that to go on in the same direction would be the worst thing he could allow as a teacher with the goal of helping me. Therefore, he went on, the focus was to be on developing the substance or "real stuff" of the Boxing. It wasn't the first time I had been offended and it wouldn't be the last. This is when he decided to teach me Pakua Chang Boxing.

He began by teaching me the circle walk, the Hawk (the first animal) and the eight changes all in one week. Actually that trip was not so different as I was learning new technique and movement. Of course I learned quickly as usual and on returning for my next trip, I expected to continue learning the next animal etc. To my shock he didn't teach me a single additional part of the form but concentrated on my lack of root and undisciplined movement. In fact, it was nearly a year before he taught me the second animal of Pakua. He also had begun to duel with me (Pakua Joint Hands) and I was totally out of control and he controlled my every movement in this duel. The point of my deficiencies were becoming clear. I never quite understood how this somewhat awkward athlete could control my energy. Finally I began to understand that without root I would never begin to develop my energy. Now it became obvious that he had to slow down my efforts so that I could see what I was missing. He demanded every moment of form practice to be rooted and balanced etc. There were to be no gaps. Until he saw it, he would not teach another move. Wow, do you think this is the proper 90's sensitivity?

Can I sue?

Come Unprepared?

Time marched on and after about two and a half years of Pakua training I had about three animals memorized. I was on tour teaching seminars in the northeast and had a trip to Mr. Casey's planned at the end of the trip. I was unable to practice as I was accustomed to for the two weeks leading up to the lesson and had some reservations about the lesson because of my lack of practice.

When I arrived he sat and talked giving me crackers and tea as was the custom and then as usual he asked me to do the form. I began and while I was not worried about the movements, I was concerned about my conditioning for the form. Knowing this, I paced myself and tried to fake my intensity. I was breathing more than I should have been and when I finished, the look on Mr. Casey was one of horrible disappointment. After a long painful silence, Mr. Casey began by saying that he respected me for the distance I would travel to learn from him and that he knew that I hoped and wanted continual progression through the Pakua study, but that my performance was so bad that he honestly could not take me further since I was incapable of holding a root for the twenty plus minutes that he had just seen me move.

I would have preferred he slap me, knock me out, or torture me than the feeling of these sharp but truthful words. I knew that Mr. Casey valued the art with great reverence and I vowed to myself that I would never come to a lesson without being totally prepared in every way as to not waste his time and to give respect to the art he was willing to teach. I can say that I never did come unprepared. Perfect? No, but conditioned and prepared, yes! Sometimes we float along in life and expect to make progress. Mr. Casey didn't think it should be done that way. He was right.

NEVER LEAVE A DOUBT

Sometimes when I teach, I will demonstrate techniques or things on a student showing things lightly etc. I can't remember a single time that Mr. Casey ever demonstrated lightly. There were few times he didn't take whatever he was trying to demonstrate and take the action to a finish position. This was simply the way he chose to teach.

Often his finishes were very painful and torturous in nature. Sometimes his wife would watch, but when things got painful she would have to leave the room as she did not enjoy such things. She told me that she asked him why he had to do the techniques so strong on me. He told her that he knew no other way to get the point across. Mr. Casey did not want there to ever be any doubt that the technique he was demonstrating was not effective. There never was any doubt in my mind. I am not the student that needed a reminder, but that didn't matter to him.

When I teach, I have always thought that one should understand the logic and mental side of the technique and a student should be able to understand its effectiveness. Over time I have realized that there are many students that do not have a strong belief in the technique and that the mental side is not enough to give them the belief. When these people "feel" the technique, the eyes light up and they believe. While I don't believe this is the way we should analyze martial arts, feeling the technique gives reinforcement even though it does not prove its intelligence. Then, only practice is necessary.

PUSH FOR EXCELLENCE - VISION

With Mr. Casey's method of teaching and martial skill, a strong case was made for the greatness of the "Boxing." A vision was produced as to what one should aspire to. Mr. Casey had the opportunity to touch and be trained by some very high level people in the boxing. They passed on that high "vision" of what the boxing was suppose to be and Mr. Casey encouraged me to push for nothing but excellence. The art was not something to pittle with as one tinkers with a hobby. It is a most precious art form that required dedication and the understanding of this "vision of excellence" was the only way in which one could pass it down with any degree of accuracy.

ROLE OF PAIN AND THE MIND

After Mr. Casey was able to teach me the various duels in each Chinese Boxing style, we would free style the duel. Many interesting things might occur in each encounter, but once Mr. Casey obtained the advantage, the result was similar regardless of the type of duel we were doing. With advantage, he would often reach with one hand grabbing my hair with his special grip. He would use this action to assist in bringing me under his total control. Now the real skill was his ability to get the advantage, but that is for another discussion. When he would grab my hair, he was so powerful in his projection, the pain would occupy my mind allowing him an easy finish. Had he not had so much projection, I probably would not be finished so easily. I cannot tell you how many times this happened, but it was many. After a few years of this, I began to improve in various ways. Now the pain was still the pain, but finally it began to happen that my mind remained focus on what was actually happening in the encounter. Now he often succeeded anyway, but now I was able to mount a counter or at least the chance existed for a counter since my mind was not totally out of the encounter by the pain. I really don't know how I would have learned this without the experience of many times until I learned to refocus my mind.

There was an exception to this thought. After teaching me his method of hand projection (Yang Dar) etc., Mr. Casey would have a test of hand projection by standing in from of a person and putting his hands on the shoulders just past the tender nerves at the collarbone cavity. He would then curl his fingers into the muscles on the back side of the shoulders, digging the fingertips in and lowering his arms/body driving the participant quickly to the ground. He would then allow me or anyone else to attempt to do it to him. He would stand there with a blank look until you were through with your effort.

As I practiced on my students through the years I improved and occasionally Mr. Casey asked me if I was ready to try the experiment again. The results never changed with him although I improved with my own students and with others. It didn't make sense to me that a person could stand in front of you and put both hands behind your shoulders and drop you instantly to the floor. First, it is not a position of leverage to drop someone by strength. I had come to accept pain and I thought it would be easy just to stand there. I knew it would hurt if I dropped and it would hurt if I stood there, so what not stand there since it would take unbelievable strength to force me down. Since he was always successful and when I came to a belief that I was not just being "psyched out," I realized that it was possible to become so good at projection that you can effect another's nervous system to the degree the person has no "choice" as to his decision to drop to the ground, but is doing so because of an involuntary reflex due to the deep penetration into the nervous system. I cannot say that I can do that to someone every time, but again Mr. Casey left a clear vision as to the potential of the "boxing."

TEACHING ONE TO ADAPT

One day I arrived in Stanford to study with Mr. Casey and as usual he took me downstairs to his workout area and talked a few minutes while having tea. The place was a mess. There were all kinds of things on the floor such as shoes, boxes etc. As usual he asked me to begin doing the Pakua form. I told him that I would clean up the mess. He said not to bother because he wanted me to do the form with all the "stuff" remaining in the floor. It was very interesting as my feet were sometimes on top of shoes and bumping into objects etc. These objects were a constant reminder of my balance and changeable state as I moved.

Another time Mr. Casey had a sheet strung up taut about five feet off the ground. He wanted me to do the form without touching the sheet with my head. Obviously that was a little lower than I was use to and I was not able to make it as far in my Pakua form as usual.

PRACTICING AT MR. CASEY'S OFFICE

Mr. Casey usually didn't have to put in very many hours at his office when I came to visit him. He either cleared his schedule or as his wife told me, he could do a forty hour work week in about five. Anyway, he took me to his office in Stanford a few times. I remember once he was dressed in wrinkled judo pants and a kung fu style top. He decided to bring a single sabre with him that day. This was a sophisticated office building and I remember walking in the building and into the elevator joined by a number of people on their way to work wearing three hundred dollar suits. I noticed some unique glances from these people toward Mr. Casey as he was in uniform with his sabre in his arm. I guess they really wondered about this man that worked in their building.

Mr. Casey had a suite of offices and had a couple of people working with him. His assistant was a lady who worked in the main room which was large. This is where Mr. Casey had me practice. I remember doing the Pakua form after I had learned the entire set. I took about an hour and I would be rather warm practicing. My movements were right in front of his assistant who never seemed to be effected. She must have been use to expecting anything with this boss. I remember learning SAS-G techniques. When he would show the techniques he would do them quite strong. One of the vital point techniques I remember he finished by picking me up quickly high into the air and then dropping me. At the moment I thought I was headed for the floor but fortunately he had sent me on top of a couch. His assistant looked up, but never seemed to miss a beat. In his office I remember a technique that went into my throat about the time I was against his wall and he had me with my feet about one foot off the ground as if I was nailed to the wall. These are images that I will never forget training with this most unusual man.

APPLICATION

In the early years of my training, I was taught by other instructors what the movements in forms meant. Sometimes I could see an obvious meaning of a movement, but there were always some things that didn't make sense and the answers from my teachers were sometimes not satisfactory. Mr. Casey gave me a totally different idea about application. Two cases in point:

I remember when I first was learning Pakua one day Mr. Casey told me we were going to work on application for the first Single Change in our form called "Sun." He began to teach several prearranged techniques that showed how the action of the first change could be applied. He stopped after showing me about ten different techniques from ten different attacks. I loved it and the next day I was having trouble remembering one of the techniques he showed me so I asked him if he could show me the "seventh" one again. He told me that he couldn't remember which one was seventh and I tried to tell him what I remembered. He told me to come over to his notebook. He showed me his notes and said he was skipping around. What I saw was pages and pages of applications he had written down just on the first change. He honestly didn't know which one was number seven. To see that much application from just one change made a powerful impression on my thinking.

Secondly, I remember asking Mr. Casey once about Hsing-i and the application of metal. I was in his room at a Hilton Hotel when I was asking him this. He told me to stand up and grab his arm. On grabbing he exploded and I couldn't tell you what happened except that I went upward and then crashed down falling over one of the beds in the room. He told me that was Metal. At the time I was still technique oriented rather than energy and principle oriented. I was thinking of the standard rise/fall motion that I associated with Hsing'i's Metal and what he did was hard for me to see any resemblance. In time I began to think more on his terms which was energy related. In order to understand Metal, I was going to have to understand the energy of Metal before worrying about any techniques. Many techniques could be Metal.

Of course everyone wants to understand the meaning of every move and action in their art, but the thinking of the boxing mind is that every part of the body is capable of throwing force and any movement can be several applications depending on the need and direction of emphasis. Wang Shu Shen was asked one day if he would explain the meaning of a particular move. He responded by asking the person what the technique could not do. He believed the answer would be much simpler. Every movement can do many things depending on the need. We are only dealing with motion and energy and the changeable "boxing" is ever loaded for action.

The most meaningful aspect of applications to me come from the process of dueling. As one develops the skills necessary in our boxing, the effort in the duels is in reacting with the instincts that fulfill the theory of the boxing. When dueling things sometime happen and upon later reflection I would realize that the response reminded me of a motion in my form. This is the kind of application that is most meaningful because it happened out of following the theory rather than trying to make a technique happen by force or thought. Needless to say, Mr. Casey expanded by thinking in this area.

APPARATUS

Another interesting lesson involved the topic of apparatus. One day Mr. Casey was teaching me the kicking board on his Kai Sai Kung Fu Curriculum. He came to a kick we call the "spring hip kick." This kick is executed at close range when your right leg is close to and behind the opponent's left leg. The opponent's knee is already slightly bent. Mr. Casey would flip his right heel upward turning his body left and crash his body weight downward leading with the center of his right shin on top of the left calf of the opponent's leg. This would drive the opponent's knee into the ground as well as cause him to turn his back even more.

After teaching and demonstrating the kick he went into something of a frenzy as he suddenly decided to build an apparatus to assist in the development of the kick. He grabbed a two by four and his power saw and cut it a certain length. He grabbed a rope and cut it into three sizes. He grabbed his power drill and drilled a hole into the center of the two by four. He drilled a hole in both ends of the two by four. He tied a rope to each end and a longer one to the center hole of the two by four. He tied the other end of this rope to the ceiling to a ring he had attacked to the ceiling. He then grabbed a fifteen pound weight and tied it to a rope hanging from one end of the two by four and a ninety pound weight to the other rope at the other end. The two by four was hanging about two feet off the ground horizontally. He then padded the half of the two by four that was closest to the fifteen pound weight. He fiddled with his creation for a little bit and then began crashing this kick down on the padded area of the two by four. When he landed the weight correctly it would lift the ninety pound weight up in the air and then it would crash down to the floor.

He could have crashed this kick down into any type of apparatus, but his mind was thinking about the energy of using this kick. When one is crashing on top of the opponent's calf it is possible that one may not be centered when the power drops and it is possible one could fall to the floor when missing and hurt one's own knee. By making this apparatus, one could start this kick and if the balance was not good, the two by four would move and turn causing one to feel the balance and change appropriately or fall to the ground possibly injured.

Mr. Casey did thinks like this on the spur of the moment and to watch his genius in action was truly a great privilege. He was so married to the theory of the boxing his creations were always in harmony with the development he was after.

To develop any technique it must be used in the air, on a human, and on an apparatus to get the full development. When we do it in the air it reminds us that we cannot lean on a target, but must be independently balance at all times if we are to be changeable and loaded. When we hit an apparatus it develops the technique for power and our body's response to impact. Thirdly, we need to be careful, but do it on a person to get a more realistic idea of the effect of the technique and the response of the opponent to the technique. Without the full development the student is surely in for surprises ahead.

STRENGTH

When Mr. Casey was teaching me the Wing Chun and White Crane butterfly knives he wanted us to get some detergent jugs that had a handle that would fit comfortably in our hands. These jugs were to be filled with water to make them heavy. We were to do an exercise in which we stepped forward while using the body to cause the arms to move in an upward figure eight pattern. The heavy jugs were to be used so that we could not easily bend our elbow which would tend to allow us to use our upper body rather than our lower body to create the pattern.

One of my students decided to make a pair of butterfly knives that were very thick and made of iron. This would give a better feel during this same exercise. When I showed Mr. Casey the knives he loved them and wanted to keep them to practice. About six months later I was back in Connecticut for another lesson. I noticed the knives had some foam and tape on them. I asked Mr. Casey about the knives and he proceeded to pick them up and to demonstrate. First he demonstrated the exercise that he had taught us to practice. Then he began to do the figure eight movements without footwork and using his waist. Finally he actually performed the Wing Chun form using these knives.

I realize the reader cannot fully appreciate the difficulty of what this means without feeling the weight of these knives, but I can tell you that I could not bend my elbows when I would hold both knives. Mr. Casey's strength was not only notable, but his ability to move his body unitarily with such a weight was truly amazing to me.

A DEVASTATING DEMONSTRATION OF POWER MOOK

One time in Stanford I was visiting Mr. Casey and he asked me how my Mook pounding was developing. I told him it was OK and he invited me to show him. There were six pounding exercises that he had taught me and I began to do them one by one. He let me continue for about three or four minutes.

When I was through, he walked over and put on a little bit of jow on his arms and mentioned that he wanted me to watch him hit the Mook. What I was about to see was the most amazing demonstration of power in the martial arts I have ever seen. He began to do the same exercise I had done except very differently. He was hitting a fast rate of speed as if doing a continual combination. He was hitting so hard that the Mook was cracking like thunder and lightening. He was hitting so hard I thought he would surely stop within a minute or two. He continued on and on and on. I was stunned at the power but continued to be amazed as this demonstration was to continue for a total of twenty minutes. When he was finished, he began to talk and teach about projection and power. He was not out of breath. He had a light sweat and I was looking at his fair colored skin because I expected his arms to be black and blue from the beating I had just seen. I was with Mr. Casey three more days and His arms were not even slightly discolored or bruised.

That day I saw the most destructive human demonstration I have ever seen. It was the scariest human force I have ever seen exhibited. Again the vision of the excellence that I have witnessed will always keep me striving for an idea that is a very high standard. I cannot demonstrate with the same level of my teacher so I have to teach one to *imagine* in order to get one to set the sights high enough for this level of the boxing.

QUESTIONS

Mr. Casey liked lots of feedback. He would ask me what I thought of the lesson. He would ask me what I thought of his technique, his teaching, his ideas etc. He did not like questions that were automated. He believed that most people ask questions only to get reinforcement for something they already believe. Once Mr. Casey came to Chattanooga and we were having a question/answer session at my house. One student asked about chi. Mr. Casey was very unhappy with the question which at the time I didn't under- stand. Later he told me it was asked as a reporter ask questions. Not to learn but as a sceptic who had his mind already set.

Mr. Casey did not try to teach in the easiest possibly way. He taught in a way that would cause one to work and go find the answers. His writings presented in this book illustrate the point. His writing is not the easiest reading. The more you know about the total picture the easier one can understand what Mr. Casey is talking about. Mr. Casey liked to teach the same truth in a variety of ways. Finding new ways or unusual ways seemed to interest him. Someone who practically knew the dictionary by heart was bored with the ordinary and always tried to express and teach in a creative way. It was not always the simple way, but he felt if one had the desire, he could find the truth.

Many times when asking questions to Mr. Casey he employed a teaching technique that I have always liked. When the person asking the question had a greater need then the answer to the specific question, Mr. Casey would answer by speaking about a topic that the person needed. While this method can be a bit frustrating for the student, it is just the method that will cause some students to begin to prioritize correct thinking related to the boxing.

FORM VS. SUBSTANCE

Mr. Casey always emphasized quality rather than quantity and substance over form. He told me once that if one knew the actual time he spent with some of his teachers, they would wonder how he could have learned so much etc.

The boxing and what it meant was what was special to Mr. Casey. He said he use to go to his teachers in hope of learning this or that in the curriculum etc. When he came to understand what the boxing was, he didn't care what was being taught as long as it was the "boxing." He would say that the last move in Bill Jee (the third Wing Chun solo form) was no more important than the first move of Shaolin Tao (the first Wing Chun solo form). If it was taught with the boxing it was worth it. He would say that you could tell a boxer by the way he walked.

This love and high standard of the boxing also brought with it an intolerance for poor martial art. Once Mr. Casey was taken to a demonstration overseas and the quality of the performances were so poor that Mr. Casey turned to his wife and said he had to leave. He got physically sick from the experience.

The stories and experiences with Mr. Casey were many and I could go on and on, but I have written this chapter so that the reader may get a little glimpse at truly a great martial artist and thinker. I don't think there was or will be many like him. I am grateful for the "gift" of the experience.

With the clear vision of the greatness of Chinese Boxing, it also took a clear commitment if one is to taste of this art. He thought that most people were in love with the "idea" of falling in love with the martial arts. Our fantasy is to be something but we don't always do what is necessary to achieve our expectations. Casey described his own commitment as "obsession."

Probably most of us will not be a Mr. Casey, but we should be clear in understanding the reasons why, the least of which is not the subject and degree of commitment.

ACKNOWLEDGMENTS

There are too many students to thank and acknowledge, but I have been very blessed to have many great and memorable students. Some were dedicated to the art, and others were big supporters of everything in which I was involved with martial arts. People have also helped me financially for various things at times. I am indebted to many people, and I am truly thankful.

My family is truly my joy, and I have also been blessed with a wonderful wife (Sharon), a son (Jason) and two daughters (Carla & Meredith). Jason and Lindsay have given us four grandkids (Josie, Leala, Ruth and Charlie) and Carla and Jeff have given us three granddaughters (Christine, Danielle and Michelle). It has been a joy to watch the direction and development of each one of them. They are all dedicated to being a follower of Christ.

With the worldview that I expressed in the last chapter, it is obvious that in anything I do, I should be thankful to God, who I believe is the Creator of the universe and the One that even gives me the breath to live. I am thankful for each day He gives me to live. The future may be difficult and some times may be easy, but I trust God to care for me throughout it all. And I look forward to my future meeting with Him in person.

ABOUT THE AUTHOR

James Cravens has been married to his wife Sharon for almost 50 years and has three grown children. He graduated from Temple University in Chattanooga, Tennessee, in 1975 with a BS in Secondary Education and a minor in Bible. He taught two years in Junior High School and began a family. After working other jobs, James decided to make his martial art business his full-time career in 1988. He has been the President of Chinese Boxing Institute International since 1981. He trains instructors for CBII and has an online Academy with hundreds of instructional videos.

James has written books on "Walu" the Bridge Art, "Chinese Boxing Synthesis" and part of another book called "the boxing." This is his fourth writing, a walk through the steps in his martial art journey. He has produced a couple dozen commercial dvd's as well as a couple thousand videos for student training projects. James continues to coach Chinese Boxing and teaches Tai Chi to seniors. You can contact him through jcravens@jcravensmartialarts.com or cbii.kaisai.llc@gmail.com.

www.ingramcontent.com/pod-product-compliance
Lightning Source LLC
Chambersburg PA
CBHW020650230426
43665CB00008B/383